SCENE OF "CONFUSION"

THE INTERIOR OF THE STOCK EXCHANGE
AT AMSTERDAM AS IT LOOKED IN THE SEVENTEENTH CENTURY

A painting by Job Berckheyde (1630–1693)
Reproduced through the courtesy of the Rijksmuseum, Amsterdam

This building, situated on the River Amstel, was opened in 1611. Trading was carried on in the open inner court which was surrounded by a portico supported by forty-one columns.

CONFUSION
DE CONFUSIONES

JOSEPH DE LA VEGA

1688

Portions Descriptive of the Amsterdam Stock Exchange
Selected and Translated by
Professor Hermann Kellenbenz
Hochschule für Wirtschafts-
und Sozialwissenschaften

Martino Publishing
Mansfield Centre, CT
2013

Martino Publishing
P.O. Box 373,
Mansfield Centre, CT 06250 USA

ISBN 978-1-61427-451-3

© *2013 Martino Publishing*

Cover design by T. Matarazzo

Printed in the United States of America On 100% Acid-Free Paper

CONFUSION
DE CONFUSIONES

JOSEPH DE LA VEGA

1688

Portions Descriptive of the Amsterdam Stock Exchange
Selected and Translated by
Professor Hermann Kellenbenz
Hochschule für Wirtschafts-
und Sozialwissenschaften

BAKER LIBRARY
HARVARD GRADUATE SCHOOL OF BUSINESS ADMINISTRATION
BOSTON, MASSACHUSETTS

Publication Number 13 of
The Kress Library of Business and Economics
Editor: Barry E. Supple

PREVIOUS TITLES IN THE KRESS LIBRARY SERIES OF
PUBLICATIONS

PRINTED AT THE
HARVARD UNIVERSITY PRINTING OFFICE
CAMBRIDGE, MASSACHUSETTS, U.S.A.

FOREWORD

A few words will suffice to justify the preparation of an introduction to English readers of Joseph de la Vega's *Confusion de Confusiones*. His book is the first that describes the practices of any stock exchange; it makes evident a high development of practices, with puts, calls, pools, and manipulations; and it appeared as early as the seventeenth century. Not inappropriately the stock exchange described is that of Amsterdam, a city which at the date of the volume's publication — 1688 — was still the leading financial center of the world. The book, to be sure, is hardly a systematic account of the institution; the author pursued moral, philosophical, and rhetorical objectives, and, while saying a lot that seems now to be of little value, manages somehow to leave unsaid a great deal that would be of interest for us. Nevertheless, it represents, even in its peculiar form, a really important source of information about the stock exchange, and indeed about the Dutch business world of that period. Today the original work is known to survive in only a half-dozen copies. The Kress Library is fortunate to possess one of these — the only one known to exist in the United States.

Perhaps because of its literary flavor and because of the paucity of copies that had survived, the book remained unknown to modern scholars interested in business and economic history until Ehrenberg called attention to it in an essay in 1892. Subsequently, but a good many years later, German and Dutch translations were executed in 1919 and 1939, respectively. The latter version is particularly valuable. It contains a reproduction of the original Spanish text, and it includes a long historical introduction by Dr. M. F. J. Smith who not only had the benefit of the research performed earlier by the German translator, Otto Pringsheim, but had ready access to all Dutch materials on seventeenth-century business experience in the Netherlands.

To translate the whole text of the book into English, however, did not appear appropriate. The diffuseness of the author and the profusion of his rhetorical excursions — which not only would make the material tedious to the modern reader but also would raise particular difficulties in the translation of numerous passages — seemed to dictate some simplification. In the end, only those sections were translated which give to the volume continuing importance for business and economic historians, namely, the portions concerned pretty directly with the affairs of the stock exchange.

The task of preparing the translation into English proved much more difficult than I had anticipated at the start. In addition to the several languages directly or indirectly involved, there was the matter of European stock-exchange practices, and the rendering of the description of these activities into the American idiom. The Library was very fortunate in being able to call upon the accumulated skills and learning of two scholars, both of whom chanced to have had German training: Dr. Fritz Redlich of the Research Center in Entrepreneurial History at Harvard, and Professor Hermann Kellenbenz, then at the University of Würzburg. These two combined talents went far to cover all requirements. Dr. Redlich brought a knowledge of modern European financial operations plus an extensive competence in European economic history, and Professor Kellenbenz contributed a familiarity with all the languages needed to handle the original text and the two translations with their introductory essays, and a specific knowledge of Dutch business life in the early seventeenth century derived in the preparation of his recent book, *Unternehmerkräfte im Hamburger Portugal- und Spanienhandel, 1590–1625*. To some extent other scholars also were drafted, chiefly because Dr. Kellenbenz lived at a considerable distance from Cambridge, and because Dr. Redlich and I were both lacking in ability to handle either Spanish or Dutch. Happily we were able to call upon Professor Stanley J. Stein of Princeton and Dr. Richard M. Westebbe of Washington, both of whom chanced to be in Cambridge at a critical period. In the end I thought it necessary to go outside the academic world for help. Mr. Carey J. Chamberlin, a Boston investment banker with a scholarly bias, was good enough to read through the penultimate product to see if it were comprehensible to members of the modern American financial fraternity, and if we had in fact employed the proper American financial jargon. He found several places that needed alteration. To all these gentlemen the Kress Library is greatly indebted. They all performed beyond the strict call of duty under any reasonable interpretation, and they all contributed to the final success. We are particularly beholden to Dr. Redlich and Professor Kellenbenz.

Although I am formally retired from the librarianship at the Harvard Business School and no longer directly responsible for the literary output of the Kress Library, I am happy indeed to be able to help in preparing this brochure for the printer. In reality I am merely responding to a "reasonable duty": the work on this translation was begun in my administration and I failed to bring it to a completion before the date of my official retirement. I am pleased indeed that my successor at the Baker Library, Mr. Donald T. Clark, has displayed a keen interest in bringing out this study.

ARTHUR H. COLE

Research Center in Entrepreneurial History,
Harvard University.

INTRODUCTION

Whoever comes to know Joseph Penso de la Vega's *Confusion de Confusiones* will recognize at once that he is concerned with a literary oddity. Here is a book written in Spanish by a Portuguese Jew, published in Amsterdam, cast in dialogue form, embellished from start to finish with biblical, historical, and mythological allusions, and yet concerned primarily with the business of the stock exchange and issued as early as 1688. Such a volume obviously requires a good deal of explaining.

I

Let us begin by identifying the ethnic group to which the author belonged. This was the Sephardic community of Amsterdam, the term "Sephards" being given to those Jews whose ancestors had lived on the Iberian peninsula — in contrast to the term "Ashkenasim," which was used to designate Jews of central or eastern European origin. During the fifteenth century great pressure was exerted by the Church authorities in Spain and Portugal to induce the Jews (and equally the Moors) resident there to accept Christianity. Some did, but many merely went through the necessary motions and secretly retained their earlier faith. When in 1492 the unconverted Jews (and Moors) were expelled from Spain, many fled to Portugal; but in 1536 the Portuguese also introduced the Inquisition, and the recent immigrants had to look elsewhere for asylum. Many of the purely nominal Christians, the "Christianos nuevos," as they were called in Spain, joined their more stiff-backed brethren in these pilgrimages. It is probably also true, relative to the second migration, that some of the Jews in Spain and Portugal were attracted to the cities of northern Europe by the economic opportunities there offered to their entrepreneurial skills.

At all events, the de la Vega family seems to have been numbered among the "new Christians." An earlier generation had moved to Portugal; then, perhaps after 1536, it returned to Spain; and finally, a hundred years later, about 1630, it migrated to the Low Countries. It found substantial colonies already settled on the banks of the lower Elbe and the lower Amstel, where the members could, of course, live openly according to their traditions. The first immigrants of this character had appeared at the close of the fifteenth century; the stream had increased in size in the succeeding century; and by the time of the appearance of our *Confusion de Confusiones* the Sephardic communities of northern Europe had in fact reached what was to constitute the height of their influence in that area. The major part of these colonies spoke the Portuguese language, since that was the official language of their congregations. Therefore their members came to be referred to by the Gentiles as "Portuguese" or "Portuguese Jews." However, curiously enough, those of the group who acquired literary ambitions chose to write their poems, plays, legal treatises, and other works in Spanish. Presumably a larger proportion of the educated element knew Spanish rather than either Portuguese or Dutch, or else Spanish was a language common to all these elements, whatever their native language.

In Amsterdam the Sephardic immigrants had greater economic opportunities and greater liberties than in Hamburg, and soon the Amsterdam Sephardic settlement outshone that of the town on the Elbe. However, any statement regarding the greater liberties granted to the Sephardic Jews in Amsterdam must be understood within the general context of seventeenth-century life in Europe. Church and guilds there imposed various types of restrictions upon Jewish activities. For example, an Amsterdam decree of March 29th, 1632 forbade the Jews to participate in any occupation practiced by members of the local guilds. Jews could not obtain membership in any of them. They were not allowed to peddle goods or to have retail shops. Craftsmanship was open to them only in lines that were related to the ritual of their religion, or that had not been organized into guilds. By the terms of these exceptions, they could become butchers, poulterers, and bakers, and they could find occupation in such a handicraft as the cutting of diamonds. Above all, wholesale trade in goods and shipping enterprises stood open to them. A certain number of them were allowed to practice the profession of broker, while others could engage in money lending, money changing, and the like.

Until recently, the economic importance of the Portuguese Jewish settlement in Amsterdam has tended to be exaggerated by scholars, but such ideas have been corrected by new research. The progress in their financial circumstances, the amount of their wealth at various times, and the magnitude of their largest holdings in comparison with those of the largest non-Sephardic enterprises are all well reflected in the accounts of the Bank of Amsterdam and in the registers of the tax returns of 1631, 1674, and 1743. We see from these newly opened sources that *de facto* the largest fortunes and the largest financial transactions were those of the indigenous families of the regents and patricians. However, it is true that the proportion of the "Portuguese" population which participated in the economic life of Amsterdam was greater than that of the other ethnic group. Recent investigations have also shown that the prosperity of this Portuguese people derived primarily from merchandise trading: the importation of sugar, spices, salt, dye woods, jewels, and precious metals from the South, and the exportation of Northern raw materials and particularly of valuable finished goods in return.[1]

However, there seems to have been a considerable tendency for these "Portuguese" to participate in the financial activities of the city, including outright speculation. Surely the civic regulations under which they lived at least opened the door in that direction, but there is also the fact that Jews who had had, as crypto-Christians, good connections with the markets for goods in the Iberian countries, would quite likely lose such contacts when they had returned to their original faith and had migrated to distant lands. Leastways, a contemporary of Joseph de la Vega — a knowledgeable "Englishman Gentleman" writing in 1701 in his *Description of Holland* — stated that "the Jews are the chief in that Trade [of stock speculation], and are said to Negotiate 17 parts in 20" of the main business, that of trading in shares of the East India Company. Accordingly, there is good reason to believe that

---

[1] We shall not have really satisfactory knowledge of the size of Sephardic commerce until the many documents of Amsterdam notaries preserved in the Gemeente-Archief have been made available, a work which is now being carried forward by the archivist Dr. S. Hart and his assistants.

Joseph de la Vega as a member of the Amsterdam Jewish community had satisfactory access to information about the speculation in shares in that city.

II

The first documentary trace that we have of the de la Vega family itself relates
to its existence in Spain. Isaac Penso or Isaac Penso Felix, our author's father, was
born in Spain in 1608, and at the time was living as a "Christiano nuevo" in Espejo,
a little place in the province of Cordoba. His family must quite surely have come
from Portugal, since the name "Penso" is of Portuguese or Gallego origin. There
are several villages with the name Penso in northern Portugal and in Galicia. Moreover, the name of another family from which Isaac Penso could claim descendancy
was that of "Passarinho," which is a Portuguese word meaning "little bird." Actually there seem to have been a number of Portuguese "new Christian" families that
moved (or moved back) to Spain in the course of the 16th century, especially during
those years when Portugal was a part of Spain.

Isaac Penso married Esther de la Vega.[2] Their first son, Abraham, took his
father's surname, but their second son, Joseph, who became the author of the *Confusion*, took that of his mother, after the tradition of his people. Therefore, our
author's full name was Joseph Penso de la Vega Passarinho, with sometimes the
addition of the other surname Felix. But he generally used the shortened form of
Joseph de la Vega.

The father, Isaac Penso, was so unfortunate as to have gained some experience
with the prison of the Inquisition, and he is known to have vowed, if and when
released, to return to the faith of his ancestors. When he was in fact freed, he actually
emigrated to Antwerp, where he would be permitted to carry out his vow, and
which, as late as the seventeenth century, still had a fairly large Portuguese colony,
consisting in an important degree of descendants of new Christians. Subsequently,
Isaac Penso lived for a time in Hamburg, to which other members of the family
had migrated. One Joseph Penso, whose name can be found in the Hamburg records
as early as 1647, was perhaps a brother. As to the place of Isaac Penso within the
Hamburg Portuguese community, it is noteworthy that he was elected "parnas,"
i.e., elder, for the year of 1655. Soon he moved to Amsterdam. Here he is supposed
to have been occupied principally in the banking business. At all events, he became
a well-to-do man and associated with the most respected members of the Jewish
community. He was elected to several posts, he opened his house for religious meet-
ings, he distinguished himself by his beneficence, and he participated in the establishment of one of the numerous Talmudic "academies" in which the study of
Mosaic law was cultivated.[3]

[2] They had four sons and six daughters. While two of the sons passed their lives in Amsterdam,
the others emigrated to London. All four of them became related by marriage to the family of
Alvares Vega in Antwerp. These several family ties were increased when a daughter of Isaac
Penso also married into the same Vega family.
[3] When he died in 1683, worthies such as Chacham Aboab and Dr. Sarphati de Pina honored
him with commemorative discourses, and the poet, Daniel Levi de Barrios, as well as his own
son, our Joseph, composed funeral orations upon his character and his accomplishments.

III

The date and place of Joseph's birth cannot be established with surety. Apparently he was born about 1650, possibly while his parents were still staying at Espejo, but more probably after they had moved to northern Europe. While a youth, he spent some time in Leghorn, and then established himself at Amsterdam, although also visiting Hamburg rather frequently. Soon he attracted attention by his literary talents. In 1667, when only about 17 years old, he made himself known through the composition of a Hebrew drama entitled *Asire ha Tikwah* or *The Prisoner of Hope*, which was praised as the beginning of a new epoch of Hebrew poetry. It was published in Amsterdam in 1673.

Although in his earlier years directed by his family toward the career of a rabbi, Joseph actually became a businessman. He managed his business activities, however, in such a way that he had considerable time available for writing; and in his leisure he composed marriage poems, poems in praise of princes, novels, speeches, and treatises of moral and philosophical character. He became a member of the Academia de los Sitibundos founded in 1676 by the Spanish Resident Manuel de Belmonte, and he served on its jury, a body which passed judgment on, and awarded prizes to, poems submitted to it. When Belmonte in 1685 founded a literary debating club called the Academia de los Floridos, de la Vega became its secretary. Journeys to Antwerp, where his wife had been born and where several of his works were published, to Leghorn, and possibly to Espejo, widened his intellectual horizon. His contemporaries praised his scholarship, his powers of fantasy, his talent for language and literary form.

Despite considerable scholarly research, no one has been able to establish with assurance a complete list of the works of Joseph de la Vega. In the preface to a collection of his novels entitled *Rumbos Peligrosos*, or *Dangerous Travels*, which were published in 1683, he stated that over the years he had written two hundred letters to princes and friends about subjects interesting to students of historical as well as contemporary affairs; these he had written to the grateful as well as the mournful and the dissatisfied, the lovers and the gay, the preachers, the moralists, and the poets. Among his more notable productions — beyond the drama already mentioned — were an *Oracion Funebre* for his mother and another one for his father, both of which were printed in Amsterdam in 1683. To Manuel Teixeira, the Hamburg Resident of Queen Christina of Sweden, he dedicated a speech which he delivered the same year in the Academia de los Sitibundos, while he honored the Portuguese agent Mose Curiel, alias Jeronimo Nunes da Costa, with a panegyric on the divine law of Moses. Another panegyric offered on the occasion of the liberation of Vienna from the assault of the Turks was addressed to the King of Poland, Jan Sobieski. In the year 1683, there appeared the collection of novels called *Rumbos Peligrosos* or *Dangerous Travels*, already noted. They were written after Italian models and were supposed to sparkle by reason of their new pretentious style. In 1685, de la Vega published the speeches that he had made in the Academia de los Floridos. Then chronologically came de la Vega's most remarkable product. This was the book of dialogues concerned with the operations of the stock exchange of Amsterdam, and the book which interests us, his *Confusion de Confusiones*, issued in 1688. In 1690 he dedicated a little work to King William III of England; while his last known publication, a speech dedicated to the Portuguese ambassador in the Hague, Diego de Mendonza Corte Real, bore the date of the 15th of March, 1692. Soon afterwards he is supposed to have died. He was buried, like his father, in the cemetery at Oudekerk on the Amstel.

IV

It was on the 24th of May, 1688, when Joseph de la Vega, following a custom of his time, signed a dedication to his dialogues on the business of the stock exchange of Amsterdam. It was directed to Duarte Nunes da Costa, an honored member of the Portuguese community in that city. The latter's grandfather, Duarte, and his father, Jeronimo, had rendered important services in Hamburg and Amsterdam as agents of King John IV in the years of the Portuguese restoration. Jeronimo belonged to the group of the Amsterdam congregation which, in 1673, had laid the corner-stone for the new synagogue there. As already mentioned, de la Vega had dedicated to him a panegyric in 1683. Now, *his* son Duarte (in the community called Jacob) was honored by the dedication of the book on the operation of the exchange in Amsterdam. One has only to look at this dedication to obtain a good idea of the flowery, affected style, of which de la Vega was so proud. It surpassed the usual profuseness of the writers of his time. He there wove a garland of fanciful suggestions and comparisons around the word "acciones" (stocks); he played with the word "costa" (coast), so as to allude to the addressee, and with the word "paxaro" which reminded him of his own line of ancestors. In the same style he proceeded in the prologue and finally in the text of the book. The four dialogues among a philosopher, a merchant, and a shareholder, intended to present a picture of life on the exchange, are interrupted time and again by light and contrived, if scholarly, excursions into the realms of mythology, philosophy, the Old Testament, and classical poetry. In so doing, de la Vega aimed at "a new style that imitated nobody, in order not to be imitated by anybody," but he actually went to extremes. The "estilo culto," which was his goal, turned out to have been complicated and affected, and for that reason alone lacked contemporary imitators, while for people of the present day its products are often very difficult to understand.

The author stressed in the preface to his book that he had three motives in writing the dialogues: first, his own pleasure; again, for those who were not active in the trade, he desired to describe a business which was on the whole the most honest and most useful of all that existed at that time; and, lastly, he wished to describe accurately and fully the tricks that rascals knew how to employ in that business. In this last connection his purpose was in part to warn people against entering into the speculation by acquainting them with the deceitful measures, but especially to unmask the evildoers. He compared the life on the exchange to a labyrinth, and assured the reader that he certainly did not exaggerate: what he wrote might give the impression of a hyperbole or extravagance, but it was really no more than a true description of the conditions. He called the dialogues *Confusion of Confusions* because there was no rational purpose in the activities which was not overlaid with an irrational one, no trick used by one person which others did not pay back with the same coin, so that, in this stock-exchange business, one moved in a world of darkness which nobody wholly understood and no pen was able really to describe in all its intricacies.

In view of these complexities, the literary form which de la Vega chose — the dialogue — was wholly appropriate. The hypothetical discussion permitted the author to expose the various aspects of the problem, and indeed to do so without the dullness of straight exposition. The form also fitted de la Vega's particular relationship to the materials which he sought to present. He could adopt and maintain an apparent objectivity, and yet could give expression to his own opinions by putting them into the mouth of one or more of his characters. It has generally been held that the "shareholder" is usually the vehicle for the pronouncement of the author's judgments. Actually, of course, the dialogue as a literary form had had a long history in 1688, having been utilized in the Bible and in classical writings, of which latter perhaps the most famous examples were Plato's *Dialogues*. More recently, the literary form of dialogue had been revived in the Renaissance by Petrarch, Erasmus, and others. If de la Vega had been looking at Spanish authors, he could have located examples easily, e.g., in the writings of the Marquess of Santillana, of Juan de Valdes, or of Cervantes, whose *Coloquio de los Perros* or *Colloquium of the Dogs* was (and is) a famous piece of literature. Even highly technical questions were at this period presented in the form of dialogues. One may refer to Machiavelli's *Dell' Arte della Guerra* (*On the Art of War*) of 1519/20.

V

When de la Vega published his book, the trade and speculation in stocks had not existed the length of a single century. To be sure, speculation in goods was older. As early as the middle of the sixteenth century, people in Amsterdam speculated in grain and, somewhat later, in herring, spices, whale-oil, and even tulips. The Amsterdam bourse in particular was the place where this kind of business was carried on. This institution began as an open-air market in Warmoestreet, later moved for a while to the "New Bridge," which crosses the Damrak, then flourished in the "church square" near the Oude Kerk until the Amsterdam merchants built their own exchange building in 1611.

Trade and speculation in shares first appeared there when, in 1602, the six local "chambers" for East Indian trade were united into a general Dutch East India Company. According to the official pronouncement, every inhabitant of the United Provinces had an opportunity to participate in the Company. At the beginning the rights deriving from the initial payments were called "paerten," "partieen," or "partijen," the words being taken over from the practice of "participation" in the shipping business. It was not until 1606 that the word "actie" (i.e., share) seems to have come into use. The possibility of trading in these "participations" was assured by the fact that each owner of shares could, by payment of a fee, transfer his holdings, in whole or in part, to another person. The chapter of Amsterdam subscribed more than half of the total sum contributed by the several chapters; and, with that proportion of "ownership" continuing subsequently, it was in Amsterdam that the trading in shares flourished most luxuriantly.

Only a few days after the original subscription had been completed, the shares of the Dutch East India Company were being traded in so actively that they rose to 14 or 15 per cent above par; and the tendency to rise continued until by 1607 the price had almost doubled. However, in the following year the market value fell to 130 per cent of par, as a consequence of manipulations by a group of speculators organized by one Isaac Le Maire, who ultimately were concerned with the founding of a rival French company. These early stock-market "operators" sold large blocks of shares and, in addition, sought to depress the price both by selling "short" and by spreading rumors that were unfavorable to the Dutch Company. Consequently, on the 27th of February 1610, the first edict was published prohibiting activities of this sort, especially the "windhandel," that is, the dealing in shares that were not in the possession of the seller. The sale of shares of the Company by *bona fide* owners for future delivery was allowed. In 1621, after the outbreak of war with Spain, a second edict against the "wind trade" had to be issued, and further prohibitions followed; but apparently the abuses could not be eliminated.

The volume of trading seems to have varied as greatly as the prices and the resort to "rigging" of the market. As just suggested, the first years after the launching of the East India Company witnessed much speculation. Then there was another period of brisk activity when in 1621 the Dutch West India Company was established, and when its stock also began to be traded in, while thereafter the vicissitudes of the war with Spain and the Thirty Years War kept business rather active over the 1621–1648 period. Then followed a couple of decades of relative quiet, terminated by the speculation that preceded the crisis of 1672. After a lapse of about forty years, a new decree, published in 1677, sought to protect the shareholders of the East India Company.

In the course of the 1680's, trading in stocks seems again to have increased considerably; and for the first time a rather lively public discussion of the problems ensued. In 1687 an Amsterdam lawyer, Nicolaas Muys van Holy, felt himself impelled to publish a pamphlet on the evils of the wind-business. He pointed out that there were professional dealers in stocks who were anxious to worm out the secrets of the State and of the Companies, in order to get the better of ordinary investors through the use of such "inside" information; and, in an effort to reduce speculation, he proposed not only that all sales of stocks be registered but that such sales be taxed. The author was of the opinion that the "Portuguese Nation" was playing a major part in the stock speculation, especially in the speculation in imaginary or fictitious units called "ducaton" shares — of which more shortly. However, his contentions met with strenuous opposition, and several pamphlets were published in criticism of his views. Finally, the magistrate of Amsterdam issued a decree on the 13th of January, 1689, which indeed did levy a tax upon transactions.

It was in this situation of the 1680's that de la Vega's book appeared. Internal evidence shows that the author had personal experience in the business of stock trading. At one place, he says, quite surely in a way of exaggeration, that through speculation in shares he had made fortunes no less than five times and had lost them another five times! If one is able to look through or around the literary peculiarities of the volume, he will find in it a reasonably realistic description of the whole stock market.

De la Vega makes the reader acquainted not only with the history of speculation on the exchange, but also with the various types of speculative transactions used at that time. And, surprisingly enough, we see most of the usages of the stock exchange of today already employed in the 17th century, although not, of course, always known by the same terms. Still, we find expressions such as difference, prolongation, liquidation, limits, brokerage, already in use, expressions which the Dutch with their trade and their financial dealings spread over the world. Also there were speculators for the rise and others speculating for the decline, each with their followers among the brokers.

One expression frequently employed in the *Confusion de Confusiones*, the "appeal to Frederick," has not survived; it had only local and temporary significance. It refers to an often repeated provision in the decrees above-mentioned beginning with that of 1621 — really before the time of the Stadholder Frederick Henry. (The provision *was* included in the edicts of 1630 and 1636, edicts of similar character, which were issued while Frederick Henry *was* in office.) By its terms, a buyer of a "short" contract (and perhaps some others) could refuse to adhere to the provisions of it; that is to say, he could repudiate the agreement, and his action would be upheld in the courts of law. Although there seems to have been dispute in the courts as to the variety of individuals and of business transactions that could properly be included within its protection, the intent was quite clearly to increase the hazards of speculation. In a sense, the provision of an "appeal to Frederick" might be regarded as a means of implementing and enforcing the direct prohibition upon "short" sales carried in the edict of 1610, and actually repeated in the subsequent decrees.

De le Vega gives a rather "fuzzy" treatment of these edicts, perhaps because he was not a lawyer; and this points to one of the limitations upon his book: the best that the modern reader can secure from *Confusion de Confusiones* is a "reasonably" realistic picture of the goings-on at the Amsterdam stock exchange. Sometimes de la Vega is inconsistent in his statements, whether because of carelessness (which the author of novels might well manifest) or because of "confusion" in his own mind. Sometimes he appears to exaggerate, possibly for effect, as the author of a drama might. And the course of composition of the book surely goes far to explain — perhaps to excuse — both of these characteristics. Internal evidence tends clearly to show that de la Vega prepared first a sort of manual, possibly for the use of his brothers and others of the "Portuguese nation" who had gone to London, and who quite likely wished to engage in the speculation in stocks that was then just rearing its head in that city, and that subsequently he decided to make a "literary" product out of the original screed. It is striking how, after expurgation of the cerise, if not purple passages, the remaining paragraphs dovetail one another. Possibly the version here offered approximates the original manual, although that end was not part of the initial plan. Finally the book contains some contradictions that derived from the specific circumstance that, between the time when de la Vega began and the time that he completed the writing of the book (or making the revision), a crisis had descended upon the East India Company. A lengthy passage occurs in the fourth dialogue, which narrates this unhappy episode.

On all these counts, incidentally, as also on account of the rather extreme complexities of the transactions described by de la Vega, and sometimes the floweriness of his language, some liberties have been taken in the translation. Words, phrases, occasionally whole sentences have been inserted (in brackets) in the hope of clarifying particular sequences. At other times a rather free rendering has been given of sentences or sections. The scholar will not find a literal translation of the original Spanish, nor of the later German or Dutch versions. However, every effort has, of course, been made to present a true rendering of de la Vega's thoughts.

VI[4]

An understanding of the data in *Confusion de Confusiones* relative to the operations of the stock exchange at Amsterdam is dependent upon the following explanations of statements or implications to be found on its pages:

1. The security chiefly involved was the stock of the Dutch East India Company — an enterprise that had been launched in 1602 and that had prospered handsomely. The stock of the Dutch West India Company played a much less considerable role. The company was somewhat younger than its East Indian counterpart, having been founded in 1621, and had been less successful. Also it had been reorganized in 1674, and its new shares were perhaps less easily susceptible of manipulation. Obligations of the state are mentioned only once or twice, but seemingly were regularly bought and sold. The East India Company had bonds outstanding but these are not specifically mentioned by de la Vega.

Actually the shares of the West India Company appear to have been bought and sold on a "when issued" basis. An edict of 1621, issued by the States General, asserts, "We understand on good grounds that some men have even sold shares in the forthcoming chartered general company of the West Indies, which shares have yet to be paid up, registered, and transferred, in order to be able to deliver these shares promptly after the creation of the company. This sort of action serves to nullify our authority, resolution, and good intent." This occurred only nineteen years after the formation of the first company with transferrable shares.[5]

2. The stock of the East India Company had a nominal value of 500 pounds Flemish or 3,000 guilders. It was quoted in 1688 at approximately 580 per cent. Accordingly, the market value of a share of stock at that time was really more than 17,000 guilders. Perhaps this high unit value had something to do with the development of devices for speculation alternative to the *bona fide* purchase and sale of stock.

3. When the company was launched, the stock was taken up by the merchants of several cities in the country. The merchant stock-owners in the several communities were organized into distinct local "chambers," which in turn participated in the governing of the company. Amsterdam possessed the largest portion of the total number of shares, but some of the stock held elsewhere changed hands from

[4] Because of the technical character of the ensuing section and of the desirability of rendering the material into the American idiom, I have been glad to rely largely upon phraseology supplied by colleagues in this venture, Dr. Cole and Dr. Redlich.

[5] Also it is revealing of the rapid-fire ingenuity of the Dutch that in this edict there is evidence likewise that buyers and sellers of shares in the East India Company had gotten together to "contract out" of the penalties carried in the preceding edict: they agreed to renounce opportunities to inform the authorities and get a portion of the fine.

time to time, at surprisingly large divergencies from the Amsterdam prices. But de la Vega confines his discussion almost wholly to the Amsterdam situation.

4. The elements in the market at Amsterdam were as follows: wealthy investors; occasional speculators, mostly merchants of the city; persistent speculators, either in real stock or in a lower-denomination substitute; the Bank of Amsterdam; persons who loaned money with stock as security (who may also individually have been "wealthy investors"); brokers of various types; "rescounters," for the settlement of "differences" relative to transactions in real shares, and at least one comparable individual who had, until shortly before 1688, adjusted "differences" relative to transactions in the substitute (ducaton) stock.

5. There were various types of transactions in the Amsterdam market.

a. There were sales of the real stock against immediate payment of cash.

b. There were comparable sales where the money to cover payments was borrowed from individuals, up to four-fifths of its value.

c. There were transactions in which future settlement dates were specified — that is, beyond the regular monthly settlement dates. These future contracts were seemingly used for both speculative and hedging purposes, both by the speculators and by the lenders on securities. De la Vega implies that the latter parties always hedged by means of such contracts. Hypothecation, which was mentioned as early as 1610 (in the edict of that year), was permitted to the seller presumably during the period of the forward contract.* Arrangements also were possible, and were fairly frequently resorted to, whereby the date of the termination of a future contract could be postponed, apparently by mutual consent of the parties. This action was called "prolongation."

A large proportion of the foregoing future sales were really sales "in blanco" — or short sales, as we would label them — even though such transactions were prohibited by laws of the state and of the city.

d. There were option contracts. These were at least of the "call" and "put" varieties, which have persisted ever since, where a party agrees to deliver a given amount of stock at a specified price upon "call" by the co-contracting party at a specified time, and where a party agrees to accept a given amount of stock at a specific time and price if it is "put" upon him then. (These are obviously also future contracts of a sort.) De la Vega implies at one or two points that there were likewise contracts of the "straddle" type, i.e., where one party to the contract agrees *either* to deliver or accept stock at a specified time and price; but the author is not clear on the point.

In all cases of "call" or "put" agreements, a premium was paid by the buyer of the privilege. The amount of the premium was dependent upon a number of circumstances: the length (in time) of the contract; the judgment of the seller of the contract as to the likelihood of the movement of the stock values in question; seemingly the number of such contracts being negotiated at the time; and other, not-unimportant factors.

Option contracts were utilized sometimes for hedging purposes by *bona fide* investors, but more commonly for mere speculation. The purchaser of a "call" contract (as in the case of present-day "futures" on our commodity exchanges) was not

---

*[The purchaser could also hypothecate; see below, pp. 5 and 24 — ed.]

usually interested really in acquiring the stock at the specified time and price, but in the difference between the price in the contract and that which might come to prevail in the market by the date specified in the contract. The same could be said of the person who used an option contract for hedging purposes: he was not interested in receiving or giving shares.

e. In addition there were purchases and sales of "ducaton" shares. (Such transactions were of recent origin in 1688, and actually had been abandoned in the slump that had occurred just as de la Vega was writing his book.) What this "ducaton" trading amounted to is a bit uncertain on the strength of what de la Vega actually says. Scholars who have worked on this period assert that the ducaton shares were fictitious. Yet de la Vega surely speaks of traders who had "bought large shares and sold ducaton shares" as well as of others who had "bought ducaton shares" because they had "sold large shares." Here, to be sure, de la Vega may be using the words "bought" and "sold" as a sort of shorthand for taking a long or a short position.

At all events the best authorities assure us that in such dealings the "stock" had a nominal value of a tenth that of the real East India shares. No delivery of securities was expected, of course, and the point of the whole business was the calculation of profit or loss at a monthly settlement date. Documents covering these transactions were actually executed between the parties. At the settlement day specified in the agreement, the "difference" between the anticipated and the actual values was paid by the party who had guessed wrong. The whole business was a form of gambling on the future course of the stock market, the course of ducaton values being more or less closely linked with that of real shares.

De la Vega describes how, for settlement purposes, the value of the fictitious stock was determined on the day appointed, namely, by the declaration of two respected individuals. At one point the author mentions the excitement and confusion on the exchange when this price was due to be ascertained and disclosed. Apparently an official of the exchange put a legal termination to the transactions to be included within the given period by raising a stick as a signal. Some folk wanted the raising of the stick delayed, others to have it speeded up; and seemingly the speculators gave loud vent to their respective desires.

De la Vega also asserts at one point that street-corner speculators who could not afford to buy and sell ducaton shares, did so in shares with a still lower value; but he may here have been indulging in hyperbole.

6. It is worth special note that much of the speculation was of a different character from that to which most Americans are accustomed. At least the mental construction is different. In America, because of daily settlements, one thinks in terms of actual purchases and sales, even if some of the transactions can take place only by the use of borrowed stock. In seventeenth-century Amsterdam — and indeed in all of Europe over later centuries — the speculators thought in terms of the "difference" between what one anticipated and what actually occurred: the "difference" between what one agreed to pay, to sell at, to deliver stock at, or receive it at, and what one found at the stipulated time to have become the prevailing value.

The system of monthly settlements provided a fertile ground for the development of this mode of thought, and of action. One could make several moves, could shift positions, &c., and some of his transactions would balance or "wash out" others.

The possibility of this sort of "clearing" was the origin of the "rescounters" mentioned by de la Vega. He describes these men as brokers who "make it their business to balance out or 'rescounter' the commitments [of the speculators, it seems] and to pay and to receive the differences." Although the "rescontranten" have been reported as dating from early in the seventeenth century, de la Vega's description carries the implication that the activity was of recent development. Surely the latter does not explain how such clearing agents could function in so large a market as he sometimes suggests to have obtained.

The same sort of operation was carried out by the "general cashier," mentioned by de la Vega, in supervising and recording the contracts relative to ducaton shares.

7. As already suggested, settlement of indebtednesses came once a month. For real stock, the closing date was the 20th, with actual payment due on the 25th. For ducaton shares, settlements seem to have come at the first of each month, although de la Vega at one place indicates that they came both at the beginning and at the middle of each month.

8. Balances at the Bank of Amsterdam were apparently utilized much in effecting payments. Stocks are spoken of as "payable at the Bank," and the premiums on option contracts are alleged to have been "transferred immediately at the Bank."

The Bank also maintained what de la Vega speaks of as "time accounts" for its customers. These seem to have been in the nature of quasi-official records kept in connection with the monthly settlement procedure, time agreements, and the government's efforts to eliminate short sales (of which more will be said in a moment). Seemingly a seller could demonstrate that he was not selling short by giving a proper notification to the Bank, which would retain it until payment had been actually made. Similar "time accounts" appear to have also been maintained at the Bank when the purchaser of stock was borrowing part of the purchase price.

The stock of the Company did not pass from hand to hand; it was not negotiable paper. A sale of stock or other transfer could be effected only by the appearance of the two parties, buyer and seller, at the offices of the Company, and by the entering of the proper data on the Company's books by the enterprise's secretary. (This was once also the procedure necessary in the transfer of balances held with private bankers or early commercial banks, a procedure which has left its trace in the Continental *giro* procedures, and in the wording of modern checks, "Pay to the order of" so-and-so.)

9. Purchases and sales were often (but not necessarily) effected through brokers, who were of several sorts. One division was that of sworn and free brokers. The former were licensed by the government, were limited in number, and were forbidden to trade on their own accounts. The latter were more numerous and, although not checked so closely by the government as the sworn brokers, are actually given a good rating by de la Vega.

Another division was that between brokers for the bulls and those for the bears. Whether both sworn and free brokers formed such alliances is not stated, nor is it clear why the allegiances came into existence. The circumstance, frequently illustrated, of intense rivalry between the bull and bear factions may have had some bearing, as is intimated by de la Vega, but also there could have been reason in the trading carried on by the free brokers on their own account. Perhaps the speculators sometimes found the brokers to be real allies. However, the author gives cases of brokers switching sides as if allegiances were not rigidly held.

10. Transactions were completed at various places in Amsterdam. Trading was general at a specific outdoor area near the old Dam in the forenoons, and in the Exchange building in the early afternoons. However, the author gives cases of deals negotiated elsewhere: at coffee houses, in private houses, even perhaps in bed!

11. Indeed the effective legal restraints on the dealings in securities seem to have been few.

a. A man who failed to meet his legitimate obligations could be declared a bankrupt; but that would be true of dealings in commodities, land, etc.

b. Efforts were made to prevent the stock-brokers, free as well as sworn, from dealing on their own account; the law was enforced enough, it seems, so that the sworn brokers abided by it, while the free brokers sometimes established nominally separate enterprises through which to do their speculating. On the other hand, de la Vega implies throughout that many brokers actually did speculate for their own advantage.

c. As already suggested, a real endeavor seems to have been made to eliminate short selling. The States General had issued an edict forbidding all such agreements, in the first days of stock trading in the Netherlands, as early as 1610; and this edict had been reissued from time to time. And there had been edicts issued since the 1620's allowing speculators to "appeal to Frederick," i.e., repudiate contracts of certain types.

However, enforcement was left to the market itself. No officers seem to have felt it their duty to intervene; and de la Vega gives no instance of official action by anybody, except the determination of cases in the courts — cases which were probably initiated by individuals. What happened was that any speculator who found himself over-extended in transactions which were technically illegal, could "appeal to Frederick"; and apparently some speculators did so.

But the types of transaction supposedly covered by the edicts were still uncertain in 1688; the decisions of the courts were not clear. De la Vega spends an appreciable time endeavoring to show what lines had been drawn. Clearly dealings in ducaton or other fictitious units were outlawed; option contracts were surely suspect; and even sellers of real stock would be wise to demonstrate the legality of their operations in the case of time sales, as by use of the purchasers' "time accounts" at the company offices. This sort of escrow arrangement, set up as early as 1613, was intended to protect against the "appeal" possessors of stock who chose to sell on time.

The general objective of the edicts seems to have been to prevent or eliminate artificial depressing of the market value of shares — "rigging the market" in more modern phrase — and the authorities went about it by forbidding sales by anyone of something that he did not actually possess and agreeing to stand behind repudiations of the forbidden variety of contract. A prohibition of the same sort as that of 1610 and later years had actually been used first in the commodity markets, and only subsequently extended to cover stock transactions.

VII

Finally the questions of value or significance may be raised; what effect at the time did the *Confusion* have? And what purposes subsequently has this book served? Of the first matter, very little is known. The facts that the book was written in Spanish rather than in the language — Dutch — which most of the speculators or others concerned with the stock market must have used, and that its form was altered from that of a straightforward manual into an extravagant literary piece — both these facts would surely have militated against its having wide reading or wide impact upon the ideas or legislative purposes of de la Vega's contemporaries. Possibly also the crisis that hit the market while the author was still busy with his pen, and the tax upon sales imposed the succeeding year, combined to dampen the spirit of speculation for a while, until *Confusion de Confusiones* had been forgotten. No part of it seems to have been translated into Dutch until the whole book was so treated by historical scholars of the 20th century.

For students of economic and business history, however, including those responsible for the Dutch translation of 1939, the volume has been of signal value. No other book deals as extensively as *Confusion de Confusiones* with the trading in stocks at Amsterdam, and nowhere else in the world of the seventeenth century was there so mature a business of this sort as existed then at Amsterdam. And surely the significance of the volume is not lessened by the circumstance that through a perusal of de la Vega's book one learns how rapidly the trading in stocks became sophisticated; indeed, how in a few decades the Dutch, aided perhaps by members of the "Portuguese nation," found it possible to devise both procedures and stratagems which modern operators have scarcely been able to better.

HERMANN KELLENBENZ

Würzburg, January, 1957.

SOURCES OF DATA UTILIZED IN THE FOREGOING

AMZALAK, MOSES BENSABAT, *Joseph de la Vega e o Seu Livro "Confusion de Confusiones"* (Lisbon, 1925), 16 pp.
Includes a list of Vega's writings.

——— *As Operações de Bôlsa Segundo Iosseph de la Vega ou José da Veiga Economista Português do Século XVII* (Lisbon, 1926), 32 pp.

——— "Joseph da Veiga and Stock Exchange Operations in the Seventeenth Century" (In Essays in Honour of the Very Rev. Dr. J. H. Hertz [London, 1944], pp. 33–49).

BARBOUR, VIOLET, *Capitalism in Amsterdam in the Seventeenth Century* (Baltimore, 1950), 171 pp. (The Johns Hopkins University Studies in Historical and Political Science, ser. 67, no. 1).

BLOOM, HERBERT IVAN, *The Economic Activities of the Jews of Amsterdam in the Seventeenth and Eighteenth Centuries* (Williamsport, Pa., 1937), 332 pp.

COLE, ARTHUR HARRISON, *The Great Mirror of Folly (Het Groote Tafereel der Dwaasheid)* (Boston, 1949), 40 pp. (The Kress Library of Business and Economics, Publication no. 6).

DILLEN, JOHANNES GERARD VAN, "Isaac le Maire et le Commerce des Actions de la Compagnie des Indes Orientales", *Revue d'Histoire Moderne*, X (1935), pp. 121–137.

———— "Termijnhandel te Amsterdam in de 16de en 17re Eeuw", *De Economist*, LXXVI (1927), pp. 503–523.

EHRENBERG, RICHARD, "Die Amsterdamer Aktienspekulation im 17. Jahrhundert", *Jahrbücher für Nationalökonomie und Statistik*, 3rd ser., vol. 3 (1892), pp. 809–826.

———— *Das Zeitalter der Fugger. Geldkapital und Creditverkehr im 16. Jahrhundert* (Jena, 1922), 2 vols.

JONGH, J. DE, *De Nederlandsche Makelaardij . . . met een Voor Woord van P. A. Diepenhorst* (Haarlem, 1949), 262 pp.

KELLENBENZ, HERMANN, *Unternehmerkräfte im Hamburger Portugal- und Spanienhandel, 1590–1625* (Hamburg, 1954), 424 pp.

Laspeyres, Etienne, *Geschichte der Volkswirtschaftlichen Anschauungen der Niederländer und ihrer Literatur zur Zeit der Republik* (Leipzig, 1863), 334 pp. (Fürstlich Jablonowski'schen Gesellschaft zu Leipzig, XI).

SAMUEL, LUDWIG, *Die Effektenspekulation im 17. und 18. Jahrhundert* (Berlin, 1924), 192 pp. (Betriebs- und Finanzwirtschaftlich Forschungen, II. serie, heft 13).

SAYOUS, ANDRÉ EMILE, "La Bourse d'Amsterdam au XVIIᵉ Siècle", *Revue de Paris*, 1900, vol. 3, pp. 772–784.

———— "Die Grossen Händler und Kapitalisten in Amsterdam gegen Ende des Sechzehnten und Während des Siebzehnten Jahrnhunderts", *Weltwirtschaftliches Archiv*, 46.bd., heft 3 (1937), pp. 685–711; 47.bd., heft 1 (1938), pp. 115–144.

———— "La Spéculation sur Marchandises dans les Provinces-Unies au XVIIᵉ Siècle", *Bijdragen voor Vaderlandsche Geschiedenis en Oudheidkunde*, vol. IV, 3 (1903), pp. 24–36.

SMITH, MARIUS FRANCISCUS JOHANNES, *Tijd-Affaires in Effecten aan de Amsterdamsche Beurs* (The Hague, 1919), 234 pp.

VAZ DIAZ, A. M., "Over den Vermogens Toestand der Amsterdamsche Joden in de 17ᵉ en de 18ᵉ Eeuw", *Tijdschrift voor Geschiedenis*, vol. 51 (1936), pp. 165–176.

VEGA, JOSSEPH DE LA, *Confusion de Confusiones . . . herdruk van den Spaanschen Tekt met Nederlandsche Vertaling, inleiding en toelichtingen door Dr. M. F. J. Smith; vertaling door Dr. G. J. Geers* (The Hague, 1939), 297 pp. (Nederlandsch Economisch-Historisch Archief. Werken, 10).

———— *Die Verwirrung der Verwirrungen; Vier Dialoge uber die Börse in Amsterdam. Nach dem Spanischen original . . . übersetzt und eingeleitet von Dr. Otto Pringsheim* (Breslau, 1919), 233 pp.

VERGOUWEN, J. P., *De Geschiedenis der Makelaardij in Assurantiën hier te Lande tot 1813* (The Hague, 1945), 155 pp.

Confusion de Confusiones

by
Joseph de la Vega
1688

First Dialogue

[At the beginning of the book, the merchant speaks of the emblems of Mercury, the god of the merchants, as constituting good symbols for the activities of his fellow businessmen. The philosopher, with witty metaphors based on the words "cash," "bank," and other business terms, stresses, in contrast, the tranquillity of a savant's life. The shareholder breaks in, leading the discussion to a specific form of business, that in stocks, whereupon the philosopher raises a question:]

Philosopher: And what kind of business is this about which I have often heard people talk but which I neither understand nor have ever made efforts to comprehend? And I have found no book that deals with the subject and makes apprehension easier.

Shareholder: I really must say that you are an ignorant person, friend Greybeard, if you know nothing of this enigmatic business which is at once the fairest and most deceitful in Europe, the noblest and the most infamous in the world, the finest and the most vulgar on earth. It is a quintessence of academic learning and a paragon of fraudulence; it is a touchstone for the intelligent and a tombstone for the audacious, a treasury of usefulness and a source of disaster, and finally a counterpart of Sisyphus who never rests as also of Ixion who is chained to a wheel that turns perpetually.

Philosopher: Does my curiosity not deserve a short description from you of this deceit and a succinct explication of this riddle?

Merchant: That is my wish also, because the importunities of instructions, the shipment of goods, and the circulation of bills of exchange are all so burdensome to me. This load of work leads me to look for another means of acquiring a fortune and, even at the risk of loss, to slough off these many wearisome activities.

Shareholder: The best and most agreeable aspect of the new business is that one can become rich without risk. Indeed, without endangering your capital, and without having anything to do with correspondence, advances of money, warehouses, postage, cashiers, suspensions of payment, and other unforeseen incidents, you have the prospect of gaining wealth if, in the case of bad luck in your transactions, you will only change your name. Just as the Hebrews, when they are seriously ill, change their names in order to obtain relief, so a changing of his name is sufficient for the speculator who finds himself in difficulties, to free himself from all impending dangers and tormenting disquietude.

Philosopher: And which name does he assume? The name of Philip, Leonardo, or Diego?

Shareholder: No, there is no need, in order to save himself, for him to take to his heels or, as the saying is, "to adopt the stockings of Villa Diego."[1] It is enough to refer to the name of Frederick[2] in order to escape terror and to suppress all pursuit. . . .

[1] The Spanish proverb here cited has two forms, *Tomarlas de Villadiego* or *Tomar las Calzas de Villadiego*, meaning to flee headlong. Villa Diego is a place in the province of Burgos. The Jews living there used *calzas* a kind of knee-breeches; and, so clad, they could flee readily from their Castilian persecutors.

[2] The name here should really be Frederick Henry. See Introduction.

I will fulfill your wish to be informed about the origin of this business, and you will see that the stocks do not exist merely for fools but also for intelligent people.

In 1602 a few Dutch merchants founded a company. The wealthiest people [in the country] took an interest in it, and a total capital of sixty-four and a third tons of gold [or more than 6.4 million florins] was raised. Several ships were built and in 1604 were sent out to seek adventure Quixote-like in the East Indies. The property of the Company was broken into several parts, and each part (called an *actie* [share], carrying the possibility of acting upon [or laying a claim to] the surplus or profits) amounted to 500 pounds [Flemish] or 3,000 florins.[3] There were many, however, who did not subscribe to a whole share, but took only a smaller portion according to their wealth, inclination, or expectation of the future. The ships sailed their courses without encountering windmills or enchanted giants. Their successful voyages, their victorious conquests, and the rich return cargoes meant that Caesar's *Veni, vidi, vici* was surpassed and that a tidy profit was made — which became a stimulus to further undertakings. The first distribution of the profit was postponed till 1612 in order to increase the company's capital. Then the administration distributed 57½ per cent, while in 1613 the dividends amounted to 42½ per cent — so that the shareholders, after having had their capital paid back to them, could enjoy any further return as so much velvet.

Gradually the company developed to such an extent that it surpassed the most brilliant enterprises which have ever been famous in the history of the world. Every year new shipments and new riches arrive, [the proceeds from] which are distributed as profits or are utilized in expenditures in accordance with the stipulations of the administration. (The dividends are sometimes paid in cloves, sometimes in [promissory] notes, at other times in money, just as the directors think fit.) From the founding of the Company to the date of this conversation, the dividends have amounted to 1,482½ per cent, while the value of the capital has increased more than five-fold. This treasure is compared to a tree, because it yields fruits [almost] every year, and, although during some years it has only produced blossoms, there have been other years when it has resembled the trees of Uraba[4] which display their fruitfulness two or three times a year, and which competed with the Sibylines[5] whose branches were of gold and whose leaves were of emeralds. Others call the Company the tree of the knowledge of good and evil, such as exists in Paradise, because it is kept informed of everything that happens along all the branches [of its interests]. However, I have come to see that it resembles the tree of life, because innumerable men earn their living in its shadow. And those who are satisfied with the fruits, and do not insist on pulling up the roots . . . , will admit that they do pretty well in such a business.

Philosopher: I think I have fully grasped *usque ad ultimas differentias* the meaning of the Company, its shares, its principles, its reputation, its splendor, its initiation, its progress, its administration, the distribution of profits, and its stability. But what has this to do with that mysterious business you mentioned, with the tricks you

[3] Hereafter the author's references to "pounds" will be understood to mean Flemish pounds.
[4] Uraba is a province in Colombia.
[5] The comment on the Sibylines may well have been taken from one of the fabulous books of travels, a type of literature of which many specimens were published in the epoch of the discoveries.

pointed out, with the difficulties you emphasized, with the entire exclusion of risk, with the changing of names, and with other exaggerations and expressions which have filled me with perplexity, rapture, and confusion? . . .

Shareholder: [Let me return to my assertions] that this business of mine is a mysterious affair, and that, even as it was the most fair and noble in all of Europe, so it was also the falsest and most infamous business in the world. The truth of this paradox becomes comprehensible, when one appreciates that this business has necessarily been converted into a game, and merchants [concerned in it] have become speculators. Had the conversion of these merchants into speculators been the only change, the harm would have been bearable, but, what is worse, a portion of the stock brokers have become card-sharpers and, though they are familiar with the blossoms, they nevertheless lose the fruits.[6]

For a better understanding of this notable fact, it should be observed that three classes of men are to be distinguished on the stock exchange. The princes of business belong to the first class, the merchants to the second, and the speculators to the last.

Every year the financial lords and the big capitalists enjoy the dividends from the shares that they have inherited or have bought with money of their own. They do not care about movements in the price of the stock. Since their interest lies not in the sale of the stock but in the revenues secured through the dividends, the higher value of the shares forms only an imaginary enjoyment for them, arising from the reflection . . . that they could in truth obtain a high price if they were to sell their shares.

The second class is formed by merchants who buy a share (of 500 pounds) and have it transferred on their name (because they are expecting favorable news from India or of a peace treaty in Europe). They sell these shares when their anticipations come true and when the price rises. Or they buy shares against cash, but try to sell them immediately for delivery at a later date, when the price will be higher (i.e., for which date a higher price is already quoted). They do this from fear of changes in the [political or economic] situation or of the arrival of [unfavorable] information, and are satisfied with [what amounts to] the interest on their [temporarily] invested money. They consider their risk as much as their profit; they prefer to gain little, but to gain that little with [relative] security; to incur no risk other than the solvency of the other party in this forward contract; and to have no worries other than those bound up with unforeseen events.

Gamblers and speculators belong to the third class. They have tried to decide all by themselves about the magnitude of their gains and, in order to do so, . . . they have put up wheels of fortune. Oh, what double-dealers! Oh, what an order of life has been created by these schemers! The labyrinth of Crete was no more complicated than the labyrinth of their plans. . . .

They buy one or twenty shares (the latter commitment is usually called a "regiment"), and when the twentieth of the month approaches (the date of delivery), there are only three possible means of settlement. First there is the sale of the shares, through which profit or loss will arise according to the purchase-price; then there is the hypothecation of the shares to four-fifths of their value (which is done even

---

[6] Here the author is indulging in a play on words, since in Spanish *flor* means both "flower," and a "trick" of a card-sharp.

by the wealthiest traders without harm to their credit); and, finally, the buyer may have the shares transferred to his name and make the purchase price payable at the Bank — which can be done only by very wealthy people, because a "regiment" today costs more than a hundred thousand ducats.

When the date of settlement draws near, and if the shares can neither be taken up by the purchaser nor be hypothecated, they must be sold. The speculators for a decline in prices [i.e., the bears] are aware of this impasse and [try to] bring about a sudden fall in price in order to cause the shares to be sold below purchase-price. [Thus serious difficulties may arise for some of the speculators] . . .

Several among those who are in difficulties (immoral people, of course) know how to free themselves through the following argument: *The buyer is not obliged to pay for that which is bought; I lose in the purchase; therefore I am not obliged to pay.*

29 *Philosopher:* Ghastly tupidity, unheard-of madness, frightful folly! . . . You assert that the speculator is not obliged to pay for his purchases, but I do not understand the reason for the lack of obligation. I doubt whether he can appeal to a juridical authority such as Bartolus or Baldus.[7]

Shareholder: This is the chief point and substance of the whole business. Of such complications would not even your Thales know anything, and from your Socrates one could only learn the wisdom that we do not know anything. Therefore I inform you that Solon is not alone as the giver of good laws. Frederick Henry, too, a shining star in the house of Orange-Nassau, promulgated (with wise motives) an ordinance for these provinces, according to which he who sold shares for future delivery without putting them on the time account should be exposed to the danger (because he has sold something he does not own) that the buyer will not take the pieces at the time fixed upon.[8] When the speculators looked for protection through this recourse (which is called "to appeal to Frederick," in accordance with the name of that famous governor), the storms stopped, the attacks ceased, and the disturbance died down. . . .

Such operations take place in the deep and dangerous waters of the stock exchange, where the swimmers calculate that if the water is reaching up to their necks, they can at best only save their lives. They therefore catch at the first best straw without embarrassment and declare that the art of swimming consists in avoiding dangers. . . . [And the most amusing] thing is that, sometimes before six months have passed, those persons whose money was taken away from them make deals again with those involved in their former business transactions. The fact that money was taken from them serves to establish a credit with which to finance new business transactions, and as a means of their losing more money. When a loss occurs, the losers are expected to pay at least what they have available at the moment, and it

34 might be expected that, as the wound is fresh, there would be no new injury. But though the proverb "He who once is intoxicated. . ."[9] condemns such goings-on, emotion has greater power than the warning of proverbs; gullibility and seduction cannot in any way be prevented.

[7] Bartolus (d. 1329) and his disciple Baldus (d. 1400) were important jurists of the 14th century, still highly regarded in the 17th.

[8] See Introduction, p. viii.

[9] The author is here quoting part of the Spanish proverb, *Quien hace un cesto, hara ciento,* which has the meaning: he who does something once may well get into the habit of doing it.

I do not say that this frivolity is general, [that is, this "appeal to Frederick," and then more speculation]. There are many persons who refer to the decree [which proclaims the unenforceability of short sales] only when compelled to do so, I mean only if unforeseen losses occur to them in their operations. Other people gradually fulfill their obligations after having sold their last valuables and thus meet with punctuality the reverses of misfortune. But I also knew a friend, a strange man, who recovered from the grief of his loss by pacing up and down in his house, not in order to wake up the dead like Elias, but to bury the living. And after half an hour of such soliloquies he uttered five or six sighs in a tone which betrayed more his relief than his despair. When asked the reason of his joy, which pointed to some sort of compromise that he had come to with his creditors, he answered, "On the contrary, just this moment I have made up my mind not to pay at all, since my peace of mind and my advantage mean more to me than my credit and my honor." I assure you that at this story and at the preposterous and unexpected suggestion I burst out into such a guffaw that I almost shed tears over it. But the fact is that there are many who, . . . like Jonas, snore in the middle of danger; and that, while Adam was ashamed of his nakedness, there are men at the exchange who are not ashamed that (to the disadvantage of their creditors) they have kept hold of their money. . . .

Philosopher: I cannot deny that, in spite of my natural inclination, I would try my fortune [on the exchange] if three great obstacles did not prevent me. 37

First obstacle: I question whether I should go on board such an endangered ship, to which every wind means a storm and every wave a shipwreck.

Second obstacle: With my limited capital, I could win . . . only if I [were willing to] renounce my reputation frivolously. But to feel degraded . . . without being compensated by wealth, such a thought is vain and insane. 38

Third obstacle: Preoccupation with this business seems to me unworthy of a philosopher, and, furthermore, since everyone knows the humble character of my surroundings, there would be nobody to give me credit and to have confidence in my beard (for they would see that I cannot pay for stocks on my own account). There would be nobody to lend me money on my beard, as to Don Juan de Castro,[10] unless it were a beard of gold like that of Aesculapius in the story of Dionysius. . . .

Shareholder: Even without going into technicalities I can overcome your doubts. . . . The first danger is removed, because [I can tell you that] there are ropes which secure the vessel against shipwreck and anchors which resist the storm. Give "opsies" or premiums, and there will be only limited risk to you, while the gain may surpass all your imaginings and hopes.

In the light of these precautionary measures, the second objection becomes void. Even if you do not gain through the "opsies" the first time, you do not risk your credit, and do not put your reputation in danger. Therefore, continue to give the premiums for a later date, and it will rarely happen that you lose all your money before a propitious incident occurs that maintains the price for several years. As the contracts are signed because of the premiums and as the payer of the premiums gains in reputation for his generosity as well as for his foresight, keep postponing the

[10] De la Vega here refers to the Portuguese savant and explorer, Juan de Castro, who lived from 1500 to 1548.

terminal dates of your contracts, and keep entering into new ones, so that one contract in time becomes ten, and the business reaches a fine and simple conclusion. If you are [consistently] unfortunate in all your operations and people begin to think that you are shaky, try to compensate for this defect by [outright] gambling in this premium business, [i.e., by borrowing the amount of the premiums]. Since this procedure has become a general practice, you will be able to find someone who will give you credit (and support you in difficult situations, so that you may win without dishonor.)

The third drawback, namely, that it is not proper for a philosopher to speculate, must not concern you, for the exchange resembles the Egyptian temples where every species of animal was worshipped. In the temple of Hercules there were no flies, it is true, but at the stock exchange innumerable men try with Herculean strength to catch the Fly of Money,[11] and for this purpose many speculators spread poison and invisible threads. . . .

46   If I may explain "opsies" [further, I would say that] through the payment of the premiums, one hands over values in order to safeguard one's stocks or to obtain a profit. One uses them as sails for a happy voyage during a beneficent conjuncture and as an anchor of security in a storm.

The price of the shares is now 580, [and let us assume that] it seems to me that they will climb to a much higher price because of the extensive cargoes that are expected from India, because of the good business of the Company, of the reputation of its goods, of the prospective dividends, and of the peace in Europe. Nevertheless
47   I decide not to buy shares through fear that I might encounter a loss and might meet with embarrassment if my calculations should prove erroneous. I therefore turn to those persons who are willing to take options and ask them how much [premium] they demand for the obligation to deliver shares at 600 each at a certain later date. I come to an agreement about the premium, have it transferred [to the taker of the options] immediately at the Bank, and then I am sure that it is impossible to lose more than the price of the premium. And I shall gain the entire amount by which the price [of the stock] shall surpass the figure of 600.

In case of a decline, however, I need not be afraid and disturbed about my honor nor suffer fright which could upset my equanimity. If the price of the shares hangs around 600, I [may well] change my mind and realize that the prospects are not as favorable as I had presumed. [Now I can do one of two things.] Without danger I [can] sell shares [against time], and then every amount by which they fall means a profit. [Or I can enter into another option contract. In the earlier case] the receiver of the premium was obliged to deliver the stock at an agreed price, and with a rise in the price I could lose only the bonus, so now I can do the same business (in reverse), if I reckon upon a decline in the price of the stock. I now pay premiums for the right to deliver stock at a given price . . . ; or I may cover myself during this period, and often I make a number of successful turns instead of waiting for my luck to come up. But the receiver of the premiums acquires that payment wholly at the determined future date, even if he also runs a risk and pockets the money with fear in his heart.

[11] Here again de la Vega introduces a play on words, since the Spanish *mosca* means both "fly" and "money."

The Dutch call the option business "opsies," a term derived from the Latin word *optio*, which means choice, because the payer of the premium has the choice of delivering the shares to the acceptor of the premium or of demanding them from him, [respectively].[12] Since the famous Calepino[13] derives *optio* or choice, from *optare*, which means to wish, the correct etymology is shown here, because the payer of the premium wishes to choose that which appeals most to him and, in case of misjudgment, he can always avoid that which he had [at first] wanted to choose. . . .

Second Dialogue

Shareholder: In order that you should not come to the conclusion that the movements of the stock exchange are inexplicable and that nothing is firm, take note and realize that there are three causes of a rise in the prices on the exchange and three of a fall: *the conditions in India, European politics, and opinion on the stock exchange itself.* For this last reason the news [as such] is often of little value, since counteracting forces [may] operate in the opposite direction.

If the wise speculator is eager to correspond with India in order to learn by way of England, Aleppo, and elsewhere, whether calm reigns there, whether the business of the Company is moving forward, whether its operations in Japan, Persia, China are proceeding favorably, whether many ships are sailing to the motherland, and whether they are richly laden, particularly with spices, it has been shown that, although there are difficulties, information about them all can be obtained. But even if one possessès such information, it will not be reasonable to speculate wildly in blind trust, for, if the speculator undertakes more than his [financial] strength allows and scorns Seneca's advice that the table should not be larger than the stomach, it is inevitable that he fall over with the burden and that the world slips from his shoulders, for he is no Atlas.

Even if we assume that the news is good and correct (something which one can only tentatively establish from private letters), that the reports come at the right time, and that they announce the happy arrival of the ships, nevertheless an untoward event occurring subsequent to the acquisition of the news, but before the conclusion of the business [by the Company] may destroy this splendor and contentment. For ships can sink inside of a harbor and hopes be thwarted.

But even though everything concerning India is favorable, nevertheless one would have to inform himself also about the European conditions: as to whether no disquieting naval rearmament is being undertaken, whether alliances are causing concern, and whether other (warlike) preparations could bring about a collapse of the price of the stocks. Therefore we have seen on various occasions that one portion of the speculators would buy on the strength of the Indian news, while another sells on the basis of the unclear European situation. For, in the latter case, the likelihood

65

66

[12] Without the "respectively," this statement could be interpreted to refer to what is now called "straddling," that is the right by the payment of a single premium to choose whether to receive or to deliver. However, there is elsewhere no clear reference to straddling; and so it seems best to regard this statement as relating to two alternative forms of contract.

[13] The reference here is to Ambrosio Calepíno (1435–1511), Italian author of a Latin-Italian dictionary.

of [a profitable] return from the imports diminishes, while, on the other hand, costs rise [in Europe] with the raising of taxes. Even if there are wonderful means of learning the most hidden intentions of princes (apart from a case like the conquest of Babylon, which became known in the suburbs only three days afterwards), the commitments of the speculators change, and their decisions become uncertain. . . .

The difficulties and the frightful occurrences in the exchange business . . . have taught some precepts. . . . The first principle [in speculation]: *Never give anyone the advice to buy or sell shares*, because, where perspicacity is weakened, the most benevolent piece of advice can turn out badly.

The second principle: *Take every gain without showing remorse about missed profits*, because an eel may escape sooner than you think. It is wise to enjoy that which is possible without hoping for the continuance of a favorable conjuncture and the persistence of good luck.

The third principle: *Profits on the exchange are the treasures of goblins.* At one time they may be carbuncle stones, then coals, then diamonds, then flint-stones, then morning dew, then tears.

The fourth principle: *Whoever wishes to win in this game must have patience and money*, since the values are so little constant and the rumors so little founded on truth. He who knows how to endure blows without being terrified by the misfortune resembles the lion who answers the thunder with a roar, and is unlike the hind who, stunned by the thunder, tries to flee. It is certain that he who does not give up hope will win, and will secure money adequate for the operations that he envisaged at the start. Owing to the vicissitudes, many people make themselves ridiculous because some speculators are guided by dreams, others by prophecies, these by illusions, those by moods, and innumerable men by chimeras.

Merchant: People who get involved in this swindle [seem to] resemble the English Quakers who believe to contain in their bodies an inner light that advises them. [By your account] these stock-exchange people are quite silly, full of instability, insanity, pride and foolishness. They will sell without knowing the motive; they will buy without reason. They will find what is right and will err without [merit or] fault of their own. They will assume that the spirit persuades them, but the spirit [it seems] will sometimes be that of Ahab that cheats, sometimes like that of Saul that rages.

Shareholder: Your conjecture is incontestable. One speculator was dreaming of a statue of Nebuchadnezzar; whereupon he immediately sold his shares, explaining the dream: as the statue was overthrown by a pebble, so the business with China would be lost by the Company, and, with the arrival of the Indian ships, a collapse was bound to occur. . . .

[Another] speculator enters the building of the Exchange, perplexed and not knowing which thought is misleading him or which is right. Then he has a sudden inspiration and calls out, *Vende los Kirios.*[14] (This is an expression of the stock exchange, the meaning of which nobody understands.) He does so with no more sense than if he had observed the movement of a cloud or the passing of a hearse in the street.

Another toreador appears on the scene, earnestly trying to keep composed. He

74

[14] The Dutch version is *Verkoop de Kirien.*

wavers as to how best to secure a profit, chews his nails, pulls his fingers, closes his eyes, takes four paces and four times talks to himself, raises his hand to his cheek as if he has a toothache, puts on a thoughtful countenance, sticks out a finger, rubs his brow, and all this accompanied by a mysterious coughing as though he could force the hand of fortune. Suddenly he rushes with violent gestures into the crowd, snaps with the fingers of one hand while with the other he makes a contemptuous gesture, and begins to deal in shares as though they were custard. He buys without restraint,[15] takes as much as he can, acquires what comes his way with no other motive or foundation than that the call of a trumpet has reached his ear. And he makes a peculiar impression when he wants to turn the circumstance to advantage, since the people on the stock exchange believe that his trumpet may cause him to commit something foolish as well as something wise.

Another eases his way into the group as though he were completely calm. Suddenly he displays excitement and starts squandering shares without any reason other than taking his coat buttons between his fingers and finding their number to be uneven. If he wins, he thinks each button a rose-bud; but, if he loses, he holds the buttons to be thorns.

The speculators do not fail to seek protection against such excesses. They are very clever in inventing reasons for a rise in the price of the shares on occasions when there is a declining tendency, or for a fall in the midst of a boom. By "antiperistasis," [16] scholars understand that the opposite has the greater power. When the air struggles with the flame, the sparks come forth with greater vehemence. . . . Because [the speculators] fear a result [opposite to that which they desire] they make greater efforts to achieve a triumph.

Sometimes a quiet state of prices is obtained and the Exchange is influenced by neither favorable nor unfavorable news. . . . Suddenly a cloud appears which portends a storm. The sellers of shares rejoice and start talk about the uncertainties in the situation and the possibilities of disasters. As quick as lightning the bulls hasten forward in order to dam the inundations and to reject this reproach on their wisdom. They resemble Aeneas who at the entrance of Hades met with a host of harpies, serpents, and centaurs, but who courageously drew his sword without being frightened and without letting anxiety paralyze his audacity. The skirmishing goes on, and at last the price is higher than before the confusion, because those groups of exchange operators who, suspecting no intrigue, had not thought of fighting and had been pursuing their regular, peaceful practices, have been awakened by the attacks. With all their strength they devote themselves to the affair and find pride in holding a weak position. Thus an obstacle becomes an advantage, and the forces which had seemed destined to throw the buyers of shares into the abyss, present them merely with an encouragement.

Despite all these absurdities, this confusion, this madness, these doubts and uncertainties of profit, means are not lacking to recognize what political or business opinions are held by persons of influence. He who makes it his business to watch these things conscientiously, without blind passion and irritating stubbornness, will

[15] De la Vega uses here the phrase *a resto abierto*, after which he inserts, in a parenthesis, which is the language of our card-sharps."
[16] From the Greek word meaning "counteraction."

hit upon the right thing innumerable times, though not always. At the conclusion of his observations, however, he will find that no perspicacity will divine the game and no science is sufficient here. For as the wealthy people [on the Exchange] also look for a counter-effect when the tendency is unfavorable, and as the indisposition of the Exchange is cured in the same way as the sufferings of a leper in Asia, . . . namely, by a poisonous medicine, . . . unfavorable news need not be regarded as fatal.

It is particularly worth remarking that in this gambling hell there are two classes of speculators who are so opposed to one another that they represent antipodes in their decisions and, as I believe, in their destinies. The first class consists of the bulls or *liefhebberen* (the latter meaning "lovers" in Flemish). They are those members of the Exchange who start their operations by purchases, just as if they were lovers of the country, of the state, and of the Company. They always desire a rise in the price of the shares; they hope that by reason of good news the market will be suddenly stirred up, and that prices will rise high rapidly. The second faction consists of the bears or the *contremine* (a name which is explained by the fact that India is considered to be a mine and that this faction strives to exhaust this mine). The bears always begin operations with sales. Some of them even surpass Timon of Athens who loved Alcibiades only in order to share his mission, namely, to be the destroyer of his native country. These bears must be fled like the plague, and one must take their part only on extraordinary occasions, as, for example, to catch a *Bichile* (which is the Dutch children's word for "butterfly"). This last is an expression used to signify a chance for a quick profit, a chance that will flutter away from you if you do not grasp it promptly, and will escape if you do not bag it quickly.

The bulls are like the giraffe which is scared by nothing, or like the magician of the Elector of Cologne, who in his mirror made the ladies appear much more beautiful than they were in reality. They love everything, they praise everything, they exaggerate everything. And as Bias deceived the ambassador of Alyattes during the siege of Priene by showing him hills of sand covered with wheat and intimating to him that such a wealthy town would never surrender because of famine, so the bulls make the public believe that their tricks signify wealth and that crops grow on graves. When attacked by serpents, they, like the Indians, regard them as both a delicate and a delicious meal. . . . They are not impressed by a fire nor perturbed by a débâcle. . . .

The bears, on the contrary, are completely ruled by fear, trepidation, and nervousness. Rabbits become elephants, brawls in a tavern become rebellions, faint shadows appear to them as signs of chaos. But if there are sheep in Africa that are supposed to serve as donkeys and wethers to serve even as horses, what is there miraculous about the likelihood that every dwarf will become a giant in the eyes of the bears? . . .

Eudicus tells that in Hestiaeotis there were two wells called Ceron and Melan and that, if the sheep drank from the first, they became white; if they drank from the second, they became black; and, if from both together, they got different colors as interesting as agreeable to the eye.[17] If you wish to succeed in your enterprises,

[17] This story comes from Pliny's *Natural History*, bk. 31, chap. 9, who credits "Eudicus" without giving an identification or any further reference.

don't drink continually of the well of the *liefhebberen* because it is no good to be white; but don't drink always from the well of the *contreminers* either, for it is never good to be black as a raven. . . . In short, not always Melan and not always Ceron, but always speculate for a rise from natural inclination and on a fall only on occasion, because experience has shown that usually the bulls are victorious and the bears lose out.

The Company is like the immortal tree [of mythology] which unexpectedly [and quickly] brings forth a new branch when an old one is cut off; there is no reason, therefore, [ever] to be alarmed about the Company's situation, because it overcomes every obstruction immediately by a new development.

Follow, therefore, this signpost, and press the soles of your feet into these footprints, so that the prospects may prove profitable for you, whether you act with honest or dishonest intentions. If you act with unfair intentions, there is the ordinance of Frederick Henry in case of an unfavorable turn. An honest buyer can   90
either take delivery of the stocks or can hypothecate them; and the profit [in the transaction] is [in the end] almost certain, so that only a war (which may God forbid), and then only if it is a fierce one, could endanger the operation and intimidate us.

One has to pay attention to the different tides and to trim one's sails according to the wind. Formerly twenty speculators ruled the exchange and as the smallest circumstance had an influence, the shares fell 30 per cent because of an apprehension and 50 per cent because of a letter. Today there are as many speculators as merchants (for those playing the game merely for the sake of entertainment and not because of greediness are easily to be distinguished), and they have had sad experiences through unjustified fears. For this reason everyone watches his stocks like a jewel, and they find it extremely painful when a real loss occurs. But fearing a mere menace means to experience grief and sorrow twice, and in advance of reality. . . .

A high price of shares causes concern to many who are not accustomed to it. But   92
reasonable men need not be disturbed about the matter, since every day the position of the [East India] Company becomes more splendid, the state wealthier, and the revenue from investments at fixed interest becomes less, inasmuch as it is difficult to find ways of investing money. The rate of interest on ordinary loans amounts to only 3 per cent a year, and, if the creditor receives security, to only $2\frac{1}{2}$ per cent. Therefore, even the wealthiest men are forced to buy stocks, and there are people who do not sell them when the prices have fallen, in order to avoid a loss. But they do not sell at rising prices either [to protect a gain], because they do not know a more secure investment for their capital. Moreover, in this kind of investment, their funds can be recovered in the quickest [possible] way, since with an active state of [stock-exchange] business one can always have control of his money.   93

The possibility of quick sales increases the value of the stocks in such a manner that the shares of the Amsterdam chamber command a higher price than those of all other chambers.[18] This happens only because speculation does not exist at the other places in these Provinces. The dividends, apart from small expenses, are the same

[18] The shareholders located in the several Dutch cities were constituted into "chambers" and as such participated in the governing of the Company through the choice of officers. Shares represented in one chamber could not be transferred to another.

for the outside chambers; yet the shares of the chamber of Zeeland are quoted 150 per cent, of Enkhuysen 80 per cent, of Hoorn 75 per cent, of Rotterdam 30 per cent, of Delft 70 per cent less than the shares of the Amsterdam chamber.

The variations of the price [of the stock in Amsterdam] do not [necessarily] follow the course of the river Moelin which runs toward the East for one fortnight and then toward the West for another. Neither is there a similarity to the Persian well in which the water rose for thirty years and fell for a similar period. The fall of prices need not have a limit, and there are also unlimited possibilities for the rise. When a merchant bought a diamond of immeasurable value at Goa and brought it from India to Europe, he was scolded by the French king who asked him, "How could you risk a whole fortune on this stone?" The wise and polite answer was: "I simply had Your Majesty in mind all the time." Therefore the excessively high values need not alarm you. There never lack princes of the exchange and kings of manipulations who are enamored of the shares. Be aware of the fact that there are as many speculators as there are people, and that there will always be buyers who will free you from anxiety. . . .

The expectation of an event creates a much deeper impression upon the exchange than the event itself. When large dividends or rich imports are expected, shares will rise in price; but if the expectation becomes a reality, the shares often fall; for the joy over the favorable development and the jubilation over a lucky chance have abated in the meantime. There are natural reasons for this phenomenon. Whenever the situation is threatening, the bears generally fear the blow, and they do not dare to engage themselves. Meanwhile, the bulls are optimistic with joy over the state of business affairs, which is steadily favorable to them; and their attitude is so full of [unthinking] confidence that even less favorable news does not impress them and causes no anxiety. But as soon as the ships arrive or the dividends are declared, the sellers take new courage. They calculate that for some months the purchasers — the bulls — will not be able to expect very propitious [new] events. So the leaves tremble in the softest breeze, and the smallest shadow causes fear — and therefore no wonder that the shares fall, because they are abandoned by the one side and are attacked by the other. Clever people make skillful use of advantages that are offered by destiny . . . ; for, if a sudden change takes place, [the speculators] can hardly pull their feet [out of the fire], and when in great difficulties they can at best save their limbs. . . .

Merchant: [As I gather from your description], the terms used on the Exchange are not carefully chosen. I notice that the language there is Arabic grafted upon Greek, and that even the most experienced person needs a new dictionary to understand it. . . . There is no expression which is not as incomprehensible as God. I really thought that I was at the construction of the Tower of Babel when I heard the confusion of tongues and the mixture of languages on the stock exchange. Sometimes they used Latin words such as *opsie*, sometimes Dutch ones such as *bichile*, and sometimes French ones such as *surplus*.[19]

Shareholder: As to the confusion of tongues on the Exchange, I am not to be blamed for it. The jargon was coined by the necessities of the business, then became

[19] The word "surplus" was employed to mean the difference in values at the settlement of contracts.

customary and proved to be practical. I sell the phrases at cost price and profit nothing save the effort to bring them forward and to explain them. . . .

Philosopher: [Going back to practices on the Exchange, I have a question. You allege that when,] because of the arrival of unexpected news, those who think it propitious buy, and the others who judge it less favorable sell, it is considered particularly wise [for the novice or the doubter] to talk to the purchasers and to converse with the sellers, to weigh opinions and reasons, and to take the most advantageous course after these efforts, [in order] to do the most promising sort of business. [This contradicts propriety.] I would like to ask whether the speculators are obliged to inform me of their secrets, or whether a speculation may be based upon the hope of such a communication. When you yourself note that a fortunate opportunity is missed in the blinking of an eye, how can it be reasonable to lose time with conversations? . . .

[But, before you answer that question, let me make a few additional comments. For example, it seems] incompatible with philosophy that the bears should sell after the reason for their sales has ceased to exist, since the philosophers teach that when the cause ceases, the effect ceases also. But if the bears obstinately go on selling, there is an effect even after the cause had disappeared. Moreover, while philosophy teaches that different effects are ascribable to different causes, . . . at the stock exchange some buy and some sell on the basis of a given piece of news, so that here one cause has different effects. . . .

However, there are other activities [of the stock exchange] . . . which do not contradict my philosophy. One such action is the strong resistance offered by the bulls against the attacks of the bears, which you have so well described. The result is that the shares rise even during the greatest danger. . . . Nor am I surprised that both parties fight with words, with hands and with feet, with mental exertion, and at the risk of their fortunes. . . . [Given the situation, I suppose that I should not be] surprised that some speculators consider a certain piece of news favorable, others unfavorable. Facts are changed by emotions, and they appear to each person in a different light. . . .

Your advice to do little business meets with my approbation; its suits my temperament. Moreover, philosophy teaches . . . that the stomach cannot digest an excess of food, . . . and [accordingly] it is very sensible to be satisfied with [limited] profits, even if one does not gain all [possible] riches and advantages. . . . At the stock exchange the speculators call a failure a slap in the face. I consider him a fool who exposes himself to such slaps. . . .

Finally, I assure you that my inclination is always directed toward a rise of prices, although I will talk to the bears. They are always pessimists, and I want to keep free from biases in the heat of the battle.

Shareholder: I had decided to translate these dialogues into French so that knowledge of the stock exchange, about which nobody has written so far,[20] might become general. As I realized that many passages which were based on puns could not be

---

[20] Pringsheim in his introduction to the German translation of de la Vega states, "This assertion of the author is not quite correct, as a few pamphlets treating of the speculation in shares were published in 1642 and 1687. The author either does not know them at all, or makes no mention of them because he thinks them too irrelevant." *Die Verwirrung der Verwirrungen* . . . , p. 89.

translated, I thought it proper to add anecdotes and embroidery, and to round off both erudition and deep thoughts with an elegant and harmonious presentation. . .

145   Since the jokes at the Exchange, in so far as they are not objectionable, form a main attraction to the business, it is not out of place to mention the innuendos in a description of the Exchange. I do not wish to give offense, I only report or, to put it better, I shoot into the air, for, as the attacks cannot then be directed toward individual persons, the arrow will not hit any particular mark.

I have promised to give a truthful account and I could not do this without an exact reproduction of the facts. And when severe critics reply that the truth is not violated by those who hide it, but by those who alter it, I assure you that I should not suppress the slightest detail I know of. I am, therefore, faithful to this obligation in so far as I do not consider the matters indecent. . . .

Third Dialogue

155   *Shareholder:* Among the plays which men perform in taking different parts in this magnificent world theatre, the greatest comedy is played at the Exchange. There, in an inimitable fashion, the speculators excel in tricks, they do business and find excuses wherein hiding-places, concealment of facts, quarrels, provocations, mockery, idle talk, violent desires, collusion, artful deceptions, betrayals, cheatings, and even the tragic end are to be found. In a song Horace extols the sweet ecstasy of a fool who fancied himself always sitting in a wonderful theatre where the actors entertained him, and the intricacy of the play filled him with delight:

> *Qui se credebat miros audire tragedo*
> *In vacuo laetus sessor, plausoque theatro.*[21]

There is nothing more entertaining than to hear the comedies that can pass as a symbol of the genius of academicians.

Thus the whole stock exchange is represented in the drama "The palace in confusion," the bulls in "Much sufferings for much profit," the bears in "The wild beast, the flash of lightning, and the stone," the uninterested in "The game is an affair of fools," the skillful gamblers in "There is no life but honor"; the Fredericks are represented in "Fortune and misfortune of the name," the lucky speculators in "May God's Son grant you fortune," the unlucky ones in "Defiance of destiny." Finally I should like you to play "The eye-opener," though I am about to perform "Give all and give nothing," for, although I teach you carefully all I know, I am convinced that I give you nothing when I want to give you everything.[22]

Philosopher: Then I shall perform "What happened one night,"[23] for last night my peace was turned into unrest, my calmness into despair, my awe into mockery,

---

[21] This couplet is taken from Horace's *Epistulae*, II, 2, 129.

[22] De la Vega may here be citing actual Spanish plays. At any rate, the first five can be identified as probably *El palacio confuso* by Antonio Mira de Amescua (1570–1640), *Sufrir por querer mas* by Geronimo de Villayzán (1604–1633), *La fiera, el rayo y la piedra* by Pedro Calderon de la Barca (1600–1681), *Entre bobos anda el juego* by Francisco de Rojas y Zorilla (1607–1648), and *No hay vida como la honra* by Juan Perez de Montalban (1602–1638).

[23] Antonio Coello (1600–1653) wrote a play by this name, the Spanish title reading *Lo que pasa en una noche.*

my knowledge into ignorance, my equanimity into frenzy, my respect into abuse. A speculator cheated me; a cheater took me at my word; a betrayer stole my reputation.

There happened to be a few friends who talked of shares and gave the prevailing price as 576. To the timid they declared that the figure was excessive, and to the courageous that it was moderate. I was pleased to hear the confirmation of my opinion and, as I well remembered the advice to speculate on a rise and as I wanted to support the faction which loves the country and the Company, I sought to demonstrate my opinion by bidding 586 for a share to a bear, who was proclaiming the ruin of the state. Hardly had I made the bid, when I was told just as quickly as excitedly that the share was mine. So great was the noise, the shouting, and the laughter in which the other players indulged because of my audacity and their anxiety, that I blushed, not because of my foolishness, but from fury and shame.

The whole night I passed restlessly, thinking that they had taken money out of my purse. This morning at dawn I inquired about the value of this paper, when a scoundrel informed me (I don't know if with seriousness or merely in order to torture me) that the price stood at [5]64 and would sink very soon to [5]20. It was a miracle that I did not fall down dead or at least in a faint. . . .

Merchant: The rogues maintained that we [must have] been bitten by the tarantula [because we were so excited] and turned the conversation to the matter of "opsies".[24] They found me full of resentment, because of the vexations that they had caused our philosopher [friend], and, driven by anger, I asked how high would be the amount of the premium for delivery at [5]80 in October. One of the rogues retorted cunningly that he would not bind himself to any rate, but would estimate the premium as 20 per cent. I offered him 15 per cent, whereupon he accepted my proposition with the remark that he would take the risk as a favor to me. And whereas I was at the time grateful for this courtesy, I was informed today that the premium amounted to 9 [per cent] at most.

In spite of all this unpleasantness, however, I console myself that I did not fall from such a high roof as our friend [the philosopher], for I know what I can lose, and the difference is no more than 6 per cent; whereas he suffers already a loss of 10 per cent, without knowing how great this loss can become and how long his uncertainty may last.[25]

Shareholder: Lest you should plume yourself too boastfully, I wish to tell you that he can be freed from distress sooner than you from anger. It is an inviolable practice on the Exchange (which once was a mere usance) that the party making a mistake is not obliged to suffer for it, if a transaction, not done at the price of the day, contains an error of 10 per cent [of the par value]. In case of unexpected news, unscrupulous traders may make offers over or under the price [of the day] and try to attract buyers or sellers by this means. It is, however, necessary to get an acknowl-

[24] The merchant's use of the pronoun "we" suggests that he was a member of the group — the "few friends" — with whom the philosopher had forgathered the previous evening.

[25] The argument here seems to relate to the amount of loss deriving from the follies in the respective cases. The philosopher paid 586 for stock when its market price was only 576; so he had an initial (paper) loss of 10 points. On the other hand, the merchant submitted to a 15 per cent premium when he might have gotten one of 9 per cent; so he stood to lose 6 points by reason of his ignorance or carelessness.

edgement of the transaction, even if it is not advantageous [for the swindler] to give
the acknowledgement, as soon as the opposite party has found himself in the error.
Although the reaction of the market is [in fact] quite varied in the face of unforeseen
news, practice has introduced the foregoing definite rule. Therefore, [the philos-
opher] can not only not be forced to take the stocks at more than 576 but he can
also refuse to carry out the transaction at all. And besides since it is his first operation and because it is generally known that he is no businessman, it is easy to negate
the offer and to prevent the loss. . . .

[To be sure, there is widespread honesty and expedition on the Exchange. For
example,] the business in stocks and the bustle of the sales which are made when
unforeseen news arrives is wonderful to behold. Nobody changes the decisions which
he makes in his momentary passion, and his words are held sacred even in the case
of a price difference of 50 per cent; and, although tremendous business is done by
the merchants without the mediation of brokers who could serve as witnesses, no
confusion occurs and no quarrels take place. . . .

Such honesty, co-operation, and accuracy are admirable and surprising. But to
make payments for obligations which according to the Exchange usances do not exist,
when your credit is not endangered and your reputation not likely to suffer, — that
is not liberality, but insanity; it is not punctuality, but prodigality; not courage, but
the foolishness of Don Quixote. . . .

The Exchange business is comparable to a game. Some of the players behave
like princes and combine strength with tenderness and amiability with intelligence,
but there are some participants who lose their reputation and others who lack devotion to their business even before the play begins.

A witty man, observing the business on the Exchange, the studied impoliteness
there, remarked that the gamble on the Exchange was like death in that it made all
people equal. . . .

[I would also remark that] a twenty per cent drop in the stock prices is not large
enough to be considered a serious blow. . . . You do not have to despair and to be-
moan your fate, for, as the price may drop twenty per cent over-night, it may also
rise fifty per cent in the same period. . . .

[However, one had best never get involved in stock speculation.] It is a great
error to assume that you can withdraw [temporarily] from the Exchange or that you
can gain peace of mind when you cease to meet with the other speculators. If ill fate
pursues you persistently, it can reach you just as well in the rocks and the forests,
where lightning may strike you and wild beasts may attack you. . . . Moreover, it
is foolish to think that you can withdraw from the Exchange after you have tasted
[the sweetness of the honey]. . . . He who has [once] entered the [charmed]
circle of the Exchange is in eternal agitation and sits in a prison, the key of which
lies in the ocean and the bars of which are never opened. . . .

Merchant: I suppress my objections [to some of your ideas] . . . and ask you
only for an explanation of the meaning of "West" and "East".

Shareholder: "East" and "West" are abbreviated Dutch terms; and whereas the
"Company" we have talked about till now is called the "Company of the East" be-
cause of its undertakings in East India, there is also another company, called the
"Company of the West", whose field of activities lies in the West Indies.

The founding of this latter Company took place in 1621, and the capital amounted to between 120 and 130 tons of gold. Its trade took such an admirable upswing that the shares of West and East reached the same value, and it seemed as if the West Indian shares would become a precious treasure. But fortune changed. The cloves were lost, Brazil broke away, fortune and prosperity vanished, splendor and reputation suffered, and opinion changed so greatly that the shares were sold at 3⅛ per cent, and the sellers feared a still greater loss.

In 1674 the *Bewinthebberen* (a title which in Dutch means "directors" and is used in both Companies) proposed a reorganization of the Company in order to repair the damage and to avoid the impending ruin, [a reorganization].through which the endangered capital would be increased by contributions from the interested parties. This kind of aid was called a *Bijlegh*, and those who disapproved of the reorganization could be forced by order of the legal authorities to sell their shares; but a compromise was permitted: the shares could be transferred to the other chambers upon payment of a small transfer charge. 194

The Company had three kinds of obligations: first, there were the obligations toward the shareholders, whether the shares had been inherited from the original subscribers or had been purchased; secondly, the owners of deposits had to be satisfied, men who had left money with the Company at low interest and who, as wealthy people, were satisfied with this return of interest; thirdly, there were the outstanding bottomries or sea loans which had been taken in order to extend the trade.

In the reorganization the shareholders had to pay in 4 per cent in cash, and they were paid in new shares 15 per cent of the nominal value of the old shares. The owners of deposits had to add 8 per cent, and in return received in [new] shares 30 per cent of the nominal value of their claims. Of the sea loans, the old ones were differentiated from the new. In the case of the old ones 30 per cent in shares were given in return for cash payment of 8 per cent, while [the owners of] the more recent loans received 50 per cent in cash and 50 per cent in shares without deduction. 195

This reorganization was carried through at the cost of 70 tons of gold, and it was after due consideration that the distinctions mentioned above were made. It was just that the shareholders be favored least, because they had been interested in both profit and loss of the Company; but the owners of deposits were allowed to suffer a smaller loss of their more liquid claim, for they had only demanded a moderate interest and were excluded from gain or loss. Nevertheless, the bottomry loans were treated even more favorably, because they were of more recent date than the deposits. For this same reason a distinction was also made between the older and newer claims, as we have just reported.

As a result of these operations the Company took on new life. (There have been, however, so few distributions of profits during the last fourteen years that the total dividend amounts to no more than 26 per cent.) The price of the shares holds at 110 per cent from the hope that large return cargoes will arrive from Guinea and Curaçao. Though the contract [now to be mentioned] offers shortcomings too, people believe in a brilliant development of the business.

The contract in question (upon which are based the most important [current] undertakings of the Company), consists in the obligation of a few Dutch merchants to take at a fixed price in Curaçao as many Negroes as the Company is able to carry from the coast of Guinea. As the merchants sell the slaves again to the [Spanish] West Indies, they gain no less by this stipulation than the Company — in a business for the running of which [incidentally] an agent is stationed in Spain and on behalf of which a duty is paid to the king.

This arrangement provides the main basis of speculation in these shares, [the prices] of which could be unfavorably influenced by [political] complications in Europe because of the increased risk to the shipments and because of the disadvantage in the [then unavoidable] increase of taxes. . . .

[I should add that] although each company is interested in peace and in the security of the state, particular factors exist which affect the two varieties of shares differently and cause them either to rise or fall [without reference to one another]. In addition certain groups have been formed. (They are generally called "Cabalas." I do not know whether this name is derived from *cabal*[26] or from *cabiloso*.[27]) Through the manoeuvres of these rings, it is possible for owners of East shares to be freed from their engagements in order to strengthen their position in "West", and vice versa. If the stock exchange turns away from one variety of share in order to favor the other, and if many shares of one kind are sold against cash in order to push up the price of the other, either by purchasing the other stock outright or by loaning to other speculators through hypothecation of *their* purchases, the speculators fear a sudden fall [in the price of the first stock], and they become depressed from fear of further attacks. Therefore they speed up their sales [of this second stock]; the zest for this paper diminishes, and its price falls.

These [West] shares are not traded on the basis of 500 pounds (nominal value) as are those of the "East," but on that of 1,000 pounds. . . . [To be sure,] they were for a short time dealt in at 500 pounds although their value, if not the risk in trading in them, was much less [than in the case of East]. But certain greedy merchants demanded that the brokerage fee be cut in half (it amounted for each party to only 1½ gulden per share instead of 3 gulden for "East") and the brokers countered with a requirement that each contract should amount to at least 1,000 pounds in order to earn 6 gulden for the same amount of work. Though the fee seems at first sight to be great, not with relation to the value of the shares but with that of the facility of the contracting, so great is the loyalty of some brokers to their principals, whom they usually call their masters, and so great is their industry, their activity, their zeal, and their vigilance that the customers get their money's worth, even with the [admittedly] moderate honesty of the brokers.

But since in this business the same tricks are usual as in the trade with "East" and since the trading in these shares is equally honest and equally fraudulent, we will continue to concern ourselves with the tricks of the first line of business, which is the most common in this city and the best known around the world. . . .

Merchant: If it is not too great a trouble for our friend, I should like to hear also about the place and the ways of the exchange transactions, how business is done, for, although we know the origin, the innovators, and the confusions of the stock exchange, we do not yet know anything about the kind of business dealings or about the site of the contest.

---

[26] The Spanish word meaning "complete."
[27] The Spanish word meaning "one who enters into intrigues."

Shareholder: The business is so constant and incessant that hardly a definite place can be named where it goes on. The Dam and the Exchange, however, are the places most frequented. On the Dam, business is done from ten to twelve a.m., at the Exchange from twelve to two p.m.

The Dam is a square which is faced by The Palace [i.e., the town hall]. In Dutch *Dam* means a dyke against the floods, for at this place once a dyke had been constructed in order to protect the town against the Amstel, the river from which the town got its name, as Amsterdam was originally called Amstel Dam.

Here on this square the game begins in the morning. It lasts until the gates of the Exchange are closed at noon.[28] Then the crowds gather in great haste in order not to be fined for coming late. Thereafter the struggle is carried on at the Exchange; and even from the greatest exhaustion the weapons are not laid down and during the great excitement no recuperation is allowed.

204

The Exchange is an enclosed building surrounded by columns. (Some people lean against these columns of the Exchange which [they find to be] like columns of fire, others hide behind them as behind a cloud.) The name "Exchange" is explained by the fact that it encloses the merchants like a purse or because here everybody makes eager efforts to fill his purse. As the word "purse" means skin in Greek, [perhaps not surprisingly] it is that many players leave their skins at the Exchange. . . .

The way in which the transactions [on the Exchange] are concluded is as ridiculous as the game itself. In the Levant an agreement is made by nodding the head. Here, however, handshakes or hand-slaps are the signs of agreement. But how painful! Many strive for the victory which the blows of the hands promise and they have only to lament the blows of fate. . . .

A member of the Exchange opens his hand and another takes it, and thus sells a number of shares at a fixed price, which is confirmed by a second handshake. With a new handshake a further item is offered, and then there follows a bid. The hands redden from the blows (I believe from the shame that even the most respected people do business in such an indecent manner as with blows). The handshakes are followed by shouting, the shouting by insults, the insults by impudence and more insults, shouting, pushes, and handshakes until the business is finished. In Holy Scripture I read that one clapped one's hands in surprise as well as on festive occasions. Here [at the Exchange], however, they clap their hands together for joy as well as in surprise. . . . Some applaud the cheating; others wring their hands in surprise at the losses. They applaud as at a comedy, and they wring their hands in astonishment at the ruin [of their hopes]. . . .

208

[The philosopher interrupts to compare the shareholder's vivid description with classical paintings. Whereupon the shareholder continues:]

In order to obtain even greater applause for my presentation, I wish to describe the nervous condition of the speculators and the restlessness of their behavior at their business. I think that they have undoubtedly been given the name *actionists* because they are always in action. . . . Thoughts about their own activities have impressed themselves so much on their fantasies that [it is alleged] they deal, act, and quarrel while sleeping.

[28] "Closed" in this connection meant open only on payment of a fine.

Two of my friends slept together. The one struck the other on the head which caused a swelling. When the latter wakened his friend with shouts, he assured his companion that he had just concluded a transaction by that blow. This speculator was a second Pythagoras; the latter was wakened by a cock, the speculator by a bump, and in Portuguese both are called "gallo". . . .

When the speculators talk, they talk shares; when they run an errand, the shares make them do so; when they stand still, the shares act like a rein; when they look at something, it is shares that they see; when they think hard, the shares provide the content of their thoughts; if they eat, the shares are their food; if they meditate or study, they think of the shares; in their fever fantasies, they are occupied with shares; and even on the death bed, their last worries are the shares. . . .

But what surpasses all these enormities . . . and what is hardly believable (because it seems to be complete fancy rather than over-exaggeration) is the fact that the speculator fights his own good sense, struggles against his own will, counteracts his own hope, acts against his own comfort, and is at odds with his own decisions. . . . There are many occasions in which every speculator seems to have two bodies so that astonished observers see a human being fighting himself. If, for example, there arrives a piece of news which would induce the speculator to buy, while the atmosphere prevailing at the stock exchange forces him to sell, his reasoning fights his own good reasons. At one moment his reasoning drives him to buy, because of the information that has just arrived; at the other it induces him to sell because of the trend at the Exchange.

Merchant: We are informed about the manner, the place, and now the restless nature of the Exchange activities. Still I wish to know how the Exchange transactions are wound up, how the shares are transferred and paid for.

Shareholder: I have already told you of the three classes which take part in the Exchange. The first is constituted of the large capitalists or the princes of the Exchange, the second of the merchants, and the third of the professional speculators.

The capitalists who live on the interest of a princely fortune preserve the dignity of princes in this business. In order to avoid all the troubles connected with the transactions, they never visit the Exchange themselves, but give the orders which they think advantageous, to the broker who carries them out as best he can. Sometimes, when a decided trend prevails, it is possible to execute an order with the greatest promptness. But there are also cases where crafty men sense the direction of his purpose and inject such confusion into his operations that he can execute the order only with [unanticipated] disadvantage and difficulty.

Some of the merchants, like the great financiers, do not visit the Exchange themselves but also give their orders to brokers. They do not think it appropriate to allow themselves to be upset by attacks, insults, and shouts. In order to escape all this unpleasantness, they avoid the crowds on the Exchange. There are, however, other merchants who go to the Exchange daily (as do the speculators); and there are five reasons why, in doing so, they manifest a preference of advantage over respectability and of profit over propriety. First, they do not wish to pay brokerage fees, and so they do business directly with other merchants of their own circle, a procedure which saves them trouble and work. Secondly, they like to have the pleasure of the handshakes, for they are [cordial] people who are glad to take a hand and who make efforts to reach out their hands. Thirdly, [if they decide to use a broker,] they have the advantage of personal contact with him — a circumstance that gives them always an advantage of a half per cent more than his broker would offer a fellow broker. This is done because the broker considers the merchants to be reliable customers, whereas he does not know [even] whether he himself is thought absolutely reliable by the other broker. Again, when dealing with the latter he would receive only half of the brokerage fee, but he receives the fee from both parties at the same time when he arranges a transaction with a merchant. Fourthly, the merchants visit the Exchange to learn about the trend of values, whether prices are rising or falling. And as the whole stock exchange crowds round these influential men in order to execute the transactions initiated by them, it is very easy for the merchants to divine the intentions [of other operators], to check the news minutely, and thus to obtain advantage from the contacts. Fifthly, they believe that their minds will sense the best possibilities, because they are *virtuosi* and veterans of business and because nobody will be able to exercise better skill than they themselves.

"Look after that which concerns you" is the advice of a prudent man. People efficient in business follow this counsel, because they believe that nobody will care better for their advantage than they themselves, and that nobody will better grab hold of fortune than they themselves can. . . .

I am not surprised that there are speculators who, though free from avarice, do not give their orders to persons — the brokers — who would doubtlessly carry them out just as eagerly as honestly, and just as honestly as punctually. But what I complain of is that some such speculators, operating under the pretext of trying to please a broker, are friendly with him (without really intending to be of real advantage to the latter). They give him an order to buy one or several shares, but at the moment of execution they appear on the Exchange themselves and offer a higher rate than they had authorized the unfortunate broker to bid, whom they had thus deceived by cajolery. What is the use of giving an order, if in the same moment means are sought to prevent its execution? Is it not obvious that in case of a higher offer the shares are more likely to be delivered to the speculators themselves than to the broker . . . whom they have treated just as smilingly as falsely and just as deceitfully as cordially? . . .

We have already stated that there are three kinds of dealings in shares. But you should also appreciate that three ways of settlement are possible. First of all there are direct transfers. For their execution, the seller of the shares has to go to the offices of the Company, located in its magnificent building, and there he is required to have the stock transferred to the account of the buyer or of the lender. (As noted, earlier, even the wealthiest people make use of this hypothecation of shares without endangering their credit.) After the sum has been paid in bank money, the officials of the Bank certify that the payment has been made correctly (the whole procedure being what we call turning "a share into cash").[29] This is done with greater or less care according to the hurry of the buyer or the need of the seller for his money, — and complaints are sometimes made of the haste and sometimes of the carelessness displayed in the operations.

The second kind of Exchange business is done *on days of settlement*. By this one

223
224

225

226

----

[29] See Pringsheim's introduction to the German translation, p. 135.

understands (or ought to at least) that the stocks are to be taken up on the twentieth of the month in which the transactions [in question] have taken place, and that they are to be paid for on the twenty-fifth of the same month. But negligence, disorder, and confusion have gained ground in this settlement process, for one neither takes delivery nor pays when one should. There are brokers whom we call *rescounters*, since they make it their business to balance out or rescounter the commitments and to pay and to receive the *differences* [only]. And as there are some among these men too who seek profit in procrastination and obscurities, it is necessary in dealing with them to watch over one's advantage and interests rather than try to be polite and courteous.

The third kind of transaction takes place *at later dates* still. Here the shares must be delivered and be paid for on the twentieth and twenty-fifth of the month which is specified in the contract, unless one makes use of the mysterious prolongations of which I disapprove because they damage the credit and endanger the reputation [of the party who asks for the prolongation]. For these time bargains the brokers use printed *contract forms* with the customary stipulations and conditions of the business. On these forms spaces are left only for the names, dates, and prices. When two copies have been filled out and signed, the contracts are exchanged by the two parties; [later,] and after the establishment of the profit or loss in the business by the rescounters, they are re-exchanged by the signatories.

For the *option business* there exists another sort of *contract form*, from which it is evident when and where the premium was paid and of what kind are the signatories' obligations. The *forms for hypothecating* are different also. Stamped paper is used for them, upon which regulations concerning the *dividends* and other details are set down, so that there can be no doubt and no disagreement regarding the arrangements.

As to the unactionable feature of any speculative transaction to be settled by the payment of differences, you are right in remarking that with *cash transactions* the regulation lacks pertinence.[30] It is, however, valid in the case of *time bargains* unless the seller has the shares transferred to the time account of the purchaser within a fortnight. Then the buyer is obliged to take up the shares, or declare himself insolvent.

Though the opinion prevails generally that this regulation does not apply in the case of the seller but only in that of the buyer, this is an error introduced by bad practice. The lawyers assert that the seller as well as the buyer is allowed to raise the objection [envisaged by Frederick Henry's edict].

The public also presumes that, if the seller of stocks buys them back (from someone who had purchased them earlier), the law does not apply. That is undoubtedly an error also. (For instance), the edict does not apply when I buy a share at [5] 40, sell it at [5] 20, and declare before witnesses that the stock so sold will serve to settle the account of shares previously purchased. By this action I have declared myself debtor for the difference of 20 per cent [of the face value] which I have lost. Therefore I am not permitted to appeal to the regulation, since I have already assumed a debt; I must pay the difference or become insolvent. But if I have bought a share

---

[30] "Regulation" in the ensuing passage refers to the edict of Frederick Henry. See Introduction, p. viii.

at 40 from someone and without subsequent declaration I sell him another share at 20, [the seller in neither case really owning the stock,] I need neither declare myself bankrupt in order to free myself [from the obligation in question] nor disappear in order to shake loose; [I can merely appeal to the edict].

As to whether the regulation is applicable to *option contracts*, the opinions of experts diverge widely. I have not found any decision that might serve as a precedent, though there are many cases at law from which one [should be able to] draw a correct picture. All legal experts hold that the regulation is applicable to both the seller and the buyer [of the contract]. In practice, however, the judges have often decided differently, always freeing the buyer from the liability while often holding the seller [to the contract]. (If the assumption is true that the regulation applies to both seller and purchaser), I can rely on it if [as a trader] I have received call premiums and am forced to deliver the stocks on the day of settlement, or if, as a receiver of a put premium, I have to take shares on the day of settlement. If, on the contrary, the opinion is correct that it applies only to the seller, the regulation will be of no use to me [as a person wanting to seek shelter] when I receive call premiums, for in this case I am in fact a seller; but it will help me if I have received a put premium, as I am then the buyer of stocks. With regard to the put premium, however, there are also great differences of opinion, for, while the scholars assume that no [legally valid] claims can be made because of the regulation, there are contrary decisions by the courts, so that law and legal opinion, the regulation and the reasons for the decisions are contradictory. The theory remains uncertain, and one cannot tell which way the adjudication tends.

However, if the payer of a put premium possesses the stocks on the day of the negotiation of the contract so that he could offer to make delivery to me and to have them transferred to my account [within] a fortnight after the offer, it is unlikely that in such a situation, embarrassing though it might be to me, the regulation can be appealed to. According to the opinion of some people, it is sufficient if the payer of the premium possesses the shares on the day when he declares [himself ready to make] the delivery and not already on the day when he entered into the premium contract, in order to make all objections on grounds of the regulation ineffective.

The same uncertainty of adjudication exists with respect to the hypothecation of stocks. While it is generally assumed that, if the shares fall below the value used as the basis of the loan, the mortgagee is obliged to pay in the difference or declare himself insolvent, a few very speculative minds have argued (uncertain doubtless because of the paucity of facts to sustain their position) that if the shares have not been transferred to the time account which I as money lender maintain, within a fortnight after the start of the hypothecation arrangement, and if the shares remain in the account [of the borrower] until the date of payment [of the loan], I can raise objections [under the regulation] in order to garner a profit as well as to save myself from a possible loss.[31]

The most amusing thing and the height of fun is the view of two brokers who

---

[31] De la Vega seems to be arguing on the basis of a legal figment: because the value of the collateral had fallen below that on which the loan had been calculated, the borrower, still holding on to the shares, was involved in borrowing on a fictitious basis — and so resembling the short seller, the receiver of a call premium who really didn't have stock to deliver, &c.

peck at each other around a piece of business, for under such conditions every respect for the customer disappears, all inhibitions are gone, their voices grow more impudent, their insults more vigorous, and their handshakes more ridiculous. The one broker offers 500 pounds and the other accepts [the proposition] (which is called *Serpilladas* [32] in the language of the Exchange), or the one broker bids a specific price for the shares, whereupon the other retorts furiously, "They are yours" (which in the exchange language means "to be captured"). Whether the shares are "captured" or "stolen," the surrounding Exchange people quarrel with one another, and the inquisitive folk make such a noise that an abyss seems to open and the Furies appear to be fighting. . . .

There are two kinds of brokers. Some are appointed by the municipal authorities and are called "sworn" brokers, for they take an oath not to do business on their own account. Their number is limited, and it changes only in the case of death or through special privilege, which is seldom conferred. The other class of brokers is called "free" brokers, also "drones" . . . , in order to indicate that they snatch the honey, their profits, from the other brokers. If the free brokers were to be sued, they would have to pay a fine for impairing the income [of the sworn brokers]; but such action is taken only in cases of personal revenge, otherwise clemency and indulgence toward these brokers prevail, instead of the sworn brokers attending actively to their own interests.

There exists an infinite number of these free brokers. This occupation is [in many cases] the only recourse for impoverished [businessmen], and the best place of refuge for many ruined careers. The stock business is so lively and widespread that, though there are innumerable free brokers, they all earn a living and they need neither become robbers who eat in order to kill, nor hunters who kill in order to eat. They all live, they all make progress, they all distinguish themselves and try to substitute great activity for lack of an official appointment. They appear so faithful and concerned about their customers that they compensate by zeal what they lack in reputation, and by devotion to business for what they lack in [tangible wealth to give] security. . . .

Philosopher: [There is still another stock-exchange matter of which you have as yet made no mention.] Those wretches who on that fateful night brought me to distress, spoke of *ducaton shares*, and I will not be satisfied until you explain to me the meaning of that term.

Shareholder: Some clerks have discovered that the speculation in ordinary shares (which are called *large* or *paid-up shares*) was too hazardous for their slight resources. They began, therefore, a less daring game in which they dealt in small shares. For while with whole shares one could win or lose 30 gulden of Bank money for every point that the price rose or fell, with the small shares one risked only a ducaton [3 gulden] for each point. The new speculation, called trading in *ducaton shares*, began in 1683. For a simple mode of clearing the transactions, the aid of a man who was called the General Cashier was secured. This man put down all contracts in a book, although previously only oral agreements had existed. For every contract that was put down, the General Cashier got a *placa* from each party. [33]

---

[32] The Spanish words *ser pilladas* mean "to be taken away" or "to be packed off."

[33] *Placa* is the Spanish word for the small coin called a *stuiver* by the Dutch.

before the transactions were booked definitively, the cashier communicated with the two parties. One rarely agrees in this business to a transaction with a longer time to run than one month, because the resources of the people concerned are not sufficient. On the first day of each month when the clock of the Exchange shows one-thirty p.m., the cashier is told the price of the large shares by two impartial stock-exchange men and, in accordance with these statements, he specifies the value of the small shares. This comedy is called "raising the stick," because formerly a stick was raised by the cashier, until this custom was given up because of the noise that was made each time. The fixing of the price is followed by the settlement of the transactions (in so far as they have not been settled in the middle of the month). Payment is made in cash, and is more punctual than with the large shares, so that even the most experienced businessmen take part in this trade in small shares, for, tempted by the punctuality, they overlook the dubious reputation of the business and endorse it [by their actions].

This branch of trade has been increasing during the last five years to such an extent (and mainly with a certain group which is as boisterous as it is quick-witted) that it is engaged in by both sexes, old men, women, and children. . . . Therefore, the means devised to reduce hazards has in fact made the dangers more widespread. The speculation has been so extended that one deals in whole regiments of [ducaton] shares, as if they were matches, and I fear that some day those concerned in the business will be burnt and ruined. . . .[34]

When a mirror is broken, each piece of crystal remains a mirror, the only difference being that the small mirrors reflect one's countenance in miniature and the large ones in larger size. . . . Stock shares are similar to mirrors, at least a special sort of mirror which makes it appear that the reflected object is hanging in mid-air, or that sort that makes the viewers stiffen from amazement because, while they are looking, they see themselves flying by. Or they are like the mirror of Achaia which, when swung back and forth over a fountain, predicted for one person life and for another death. Fearful persons broke this mirror [the large "East" shares] and cut the crystal into pieces by agreeing to regard each 500 pounds of the large shares as 5,000 small ones. They intended thereby to moderate the trade, but they managed merely to make many transactions out of one, and from one mirror many. . . .

The reason why nearly all of the [speculators] participate so eagerly in the trading in small shares is the intention of the buyers of large shares to sell them as small ones, (because at the beginning of the month the price of the small shares is higher than that of the large ones).[35] As they profit by this operation, they neither dislike the labor involved nor do they consider the unworthiness of the business and its dangers.

The unwise transferring of shares from the one group of speculators to the other (which is the only transferring that these shares undergo) enhances the noise, the shouting, and the bustle that prevails on the day of settlement. (On week-days the settlement is made in the Exchange [building]; on Sundays and holidays in the main street.) So great is the noise that some folk believe themselves to be attacked; others fear to be killed. He who has bought large shares and sold ducaton shares, makes efforts to have the stick kept low [i.e., the trading continued a few minutes]

---

[34] Cf. below, regarding the abandonment of this type of speculation in 1688, p. 40.

[35] This divergence may have derived from the difference in the monthly settlement dates.

in order to reap the profit from the small shares, and to continue his engagements in the large shares. He, however, who has bought ducaton shares because he has sold large shares [short], demands the stick to be lifted up, in order to secure his profit, and will await the conclusion of his business with the large shares, hoping for yet a greater profit. . . .

Thomas de Vega describes the behavior of a fool who asked the physicians to let him swim in a lake, but when he found that the water rose up to his throat, he regained his sound mind, recovered his health, and remained in that state. Oh, how many sick persons are there in the stock-gambling who resemble the fool, who throw themselves into this sea [of speculation] and who, when the waters reach their necks, return to firm ground. But the worst of all is that they are not aware of the remedy when bewildered they plunge into this whirlpool. Of the crocodile it is said that it is the biggest lizard that grows from the smallest beginning. From the little beginning of the ducaton shares there have developed the activities of the slyest speculators; and nobody feels uneasy about it nor feels that he need apologize for it. . . .

The speculators believe in vain that through abandoning the business in large shares they can avoid their irrevocable destiny and can free themselves from the fetters of the [gambling in] stocks. But they will discover that by engaging in the trading in ducaton shares, they just prolong the agony. . . . As I pointed out before, the speculators make innumerable transactions in order that [any particular] loss will not bear too heavily on them. . . . Although one can read our losses from our eyes, we get into the business deeper and deeper. May God keep us from losing everything!

The pleasure in this gamble has grown to such an extent that people who cannot gamble a ducaton per point risk a stuiver, and those to whom a stuiver is too much, risk a still smaller coin. Even children who hardly know the world and at best own a little pocket money agree that each point by which the large shares rise or fall will mean a certain amount of their pocket money for their small shares. . . . If one were to lead a stranger through the streets of Amsterdam and ask him where he was, he would answer, "Among speculators," for there is no corner [in the city] where one does not talk shares.

The two main reasons for the introduction of this kind of speculation [i.e., that in ducaton shares] was the greed of the brokers, and the need of the other people who invented the gamble. To make it quite clear, be it remarked that there are three reasons for the greediness of the brokers, and that on these accounts many have already been ruined. First, they want to earn the brokerage fees; secondly, they wish to make quick gains [on their own dealings] out of the price fluctuations; thirdly, they wish to live in comfort.

[1] If they try to achieve all these ends [at one time], they will easily meet with failure, for, when seeking to secure a large brokerage income, they have to offer or to take large batches of stock [on their own account]; and thus they may easily be caught (or in Dutch language "hanged"). Thus they are dependent [on a flow] of fresh news and are exposed to ruin.

[2] The brokers who intend to seek quick gains through price changes, i.e., by getting large orders from their customers and speculating extensively [on their own account] in executing these orders, experience the same fate. For, although it is not

their intention to keep the shares [bought for their clients] for any length of time at their own risk, they cannot foresee incidents that may occur suddenly during this time [while they are holding the shares].

[3] He who devotes himself voluntarily to the business, in order to meet with intelligence and courage all its vicissitudes, will have the greater satisfaction, the stronger become the attacks, but in the end [even] he will have to confess that the business is such that he is always in the dark, that it is always risky, and that it is always frightening.

In order to gain from [the second] of the three methods mentioned above, the brokers must be popular at the stock exchange, for if, at the conclusion of the business, they are asked about their customers, they need the help of a good friend who will sign the contracts for them and will conceal the true character of the affair. This concealment and cloaking of the orders has spread in such a manner that even the merchants make use of the manoeuvre, although this also may prove detrimental to guileless people.

When the merchants come to know about an event which certainly will bring about a change of the price, they turn to the brokers in order to derive benefit from this change. But they give their orders only to those who will not divulge their names before the order is carried out, for it seems to them that the financial standing of the principal [giving the order] might be doubted [or] that the price might be changed before its execution. . . .

If a broker receives an order of this character,[36] he does not dare conclude the transaction lest people take notice of the order and [later] blame him for executing the deal. He is afraid of a [possible] reaction on the price or of attracting unfavorable attention. He is suspicious that by means of further inquiries one may discover who his customer is and [then] that nobody would sell the shares to him on his own account. Consequently, his selfish interest struggles with his faithfulness, his ambition with his fears, profit with conscience, until in the end the broker decides to discuss the matter with a friend, who in his own name sells so many thousand pounds of ducaton shares and thus enables him to remain behind the scenes.

Although brokers were the original inventors of this gamble, people less favorably situated entered it. To be sure, the greater part of the profits from this gambling are spent on cards, dice, wine, banquets, gifts, ladies, carriages, splendid clothing, and other luxuries. Nevertheless there are also numerous people in the business simply for the reason of providing decently for their families. . . .

Some gamble for the fun of it, some for vanity, many are spendthrifts, many find satisfaction in their occupation, and quite a few [just] make a living here [at the stock exchange]. If they are hit by bad luck and are unable to prevent their own downfall, they at least try to save their honor. They take premiums, refund the invested money, pay the differences, the furore subsides, their troubles ease, the confusion is overcome, and the attack defeated.

This [namely, the possibility of avoiding a complete catastrophe] is the reason why so many jump into this whirlpool. And it is easier to count those who do not deal with ducaton shares than those who do.

[36] De la Vega here anticipates what he explains at some length shortly, i.e., that this broker is affiliated with the party of the bulls. He also takes here the special case of an event which will have a depressing effect on the price of the stock.

Fourth Dialogue

Shareholder: In the first dialogue I dealt with the beginnings and the etymology of the stock exchange, with the wealth of the Company, . . . the considerable extension of the speculation, and the meaning of the premium business, while I made some allusion to the swindling manoeuvres.

In the second dialogue I explained to you the instability of prices and the reasons therefor, gave advice for a successful speculation, pointed out the causes of the ups and downs, talked about the fears of the bears and courageous attitude of the bulls, about the results of the bold enterprise of the latter and the significance of the timid procedure of the former, about the signs of the upheavals and their incomprehensibility, the frenzy and the foolishness of the speculation, the language used on the exchange, and the expressions which are customary there.

In the third dialogue I began to explain to you various transactions, to teach you some of the rules [of the game], and to clarify some of the business practices. I talked about the equity of the contracts, the time of delivery, the place of the transference of the shares, the location of the business, the indecent behavior [on the Exchange], the unrest, the vulgarities, the handshakes, the impossibility of getting out of the Exchange frenzy, the West Indian Company, the principles of the ducaton speculation, the types of Exchange people, the delay in the settlement of the accounts, the varieties of brokers, their conscientiousness, their risks, and their temerity. Therefore, only a description of the most speculative part of the business is now left to me, the climax of the Exchange transactions, the acme of Exchange operations, the craftiest and most complicated machinations which exist in the maze of the Exchange and which require the greatest possible cunning. . . .

278

Some ten or twelve persons [will, for example,] get together at the Exchange and form a ring (which is called a "Cabala," as already mentioned). When this ring thinks it advisable to sell shares, the means for prudently carrying out this purpose are given much thought. The members initiate action only when they can foresee its result, so that, apart from unlucky incidents, they can reckon on a rather sure success. . . .

289

They [the ring of the bears] strike the first blow with time sales, reserving the cash sales for the moment of greater distress. They sell 50,000 pounds for various [forward] months, an operation through which a decline of prices is bound to occur. The declining tendency spreads, the [ring of the] bears receives help from other speculators, and it becomes obvious that, with so broad a participation, the object [of the machinations] is sure to be achieved. The leaders of such manoeuvres can be called "Princes of the Tail," as Amadeo I of Savoy was called the "Duke of the Tail" because of his numerous suite. This expression can be applied to the leaders of the bears because of the untold hosts of adherents, or because their followers *cling* to them, or because these followers should carry their leaders' trains. As there are so many people who cannot wait to follow the prevailing trend of opinion, I am not surprised that a small group becomes an army. [Most people] think only of doing what the others do and of following their examples. . . .

293

The first trick [of the bears' ring] is the following: in order to prevent numerous extensions of the contracts by which the great financiers buy shares for cash and sell them on term, contenting themselves with [a spread in price equivalent to] the interest on the money invested, the ring arranges sales for later dates at the same price at which the shares are being sold for cash; in the hope of a greater profit, they do not pay attention to the loss of interest. They are like Aesop's dog which let go the meat because its shadow appeared bigger to him.

Secondly, a broker in whom the syndicate has confidence is given the order to buy secretly a batch of shares from an [avowed] bull, without revealing his real principal. But he sells the very same shares with a good deal of publicity, while it is shouted out that even the bulls are making sales. As the broker wants to sell to one bull the same shares he has bought from another bull, the first one sees that the story about the sales of the latter is true. Alarmed, the second bull sells his shares also. Seized by fear, everybody tries to forestall the sales of the others and regards any advice to buy as deceitful. Such a panic we call "to be in tortures," [37] and innumerable [traders] take to their heels . . . when even the slightest suspicion is roused. . . .

Thirdly, the syndicate of the bears sells some blocks of shares for cash to one of the wealthy people who live on the hypothecation of stocks. As it is known that the latter [as a matter of course] sell at once for future delivery the shares which they have bought for cash, the syndicate bids its broker [charged with the execution of the manoeuvre], before the fixing of the prices [of the day], to send a message very secretly to the agent of every business firm [represented on the Exchange], a communication which will soon be an *open secret*, to the effect that the great capitalist has received important news, and that alarmed by it he intends to sell stocks. When afterwards the sales are actually made, the swindle seems to be verified, the aim is reached, fear spreads, and a crash of prices is brought about. But the panic can easily be explained if the speculators suspect a change of opinion by their protectors and see their foundations shaken.

Fourthly, at the beginning of a campaign, the syndicate borrows all the money available at the Exchange and makes it apparent that it wishes to buy shares with this money. Afterwards, however, large *sales* are executed. Thus two birds are killed with one stone. First, the Exchange is supposed to believe that the original plan is altered because of important news; secondly, the bulls are prevented from finding money for hypothecating their shares. They are, therefore, compelled to sell, since they do not have the money to take up the stock [or else fall into the trap described as the seventh stratagem]. . . .

The fifth stratagem [of the syndicate] consists in selling the largest possible quantity of call options in order [apparently by the absorption of available loan funds] to bring pressure on the payers of premiums to sell the stocks if they exercise their right to call.

The sixth stratagem is to enter into as many put contracts as possible, until the receivers of the premiums [assumed to be bulls] do not dare to buy more stock [on their own initiative]. [Their hands will be largely tied] because they are already obliged to take the stock [covered by the put premiums, if requested so to do]. Therefore the speculation for a decline has free course and is an almost sure success. We say of those who buy by means of a forward call contract and sell at a fixed

---

[37] In the original, the Spanish phrase is *tener calcetas*.

[future] term or of those who sell by means of a put contract and buy at a fixed [future] term *that they shift the course of their speculation*. But as [the course chosen] may turn out to be the wrong [line of] speculation and the right way can thus be missed, [such a shift] is rarely made.

The seventh stratagem is to recognize that the bulls are in need of shares to survive the siege; and so [the bears] give them money. Then [the bears] sell the hypothe-cated shares again and, with the difference between what they receive on the sales and what they loan on the shares, they are able to engage in further call and put operations.[38]

This is a devilish trick, since, as it were, immortality is promised and death is given. It seems as if the bears give life to the bulls by lending them money [when they hypothecate] the stocks which the latter have bought; [but the ring turns around and sells these shares, so that the bulls have] to buy again the stocks which they had hypothecated. . . .

Although the bears lack shares, they do not blush to create the appearance of an abundance. The shares change hands, often fifty times in one week, rising and falling like balls [in a game], but this changing of hands is indicative only of the ruin of the business in shares. . . . What meaning does it have that the bears buy one share, when, protected by their alliance, they sell ten shares? What does it mean when they take over the hypothecated shares in order to pass them out again im-mediately? How can one suppress anxiety [about this situation] and how can one avoid lamentations? . . . Would scholars consider incorrect [a statement to the effect] that I cannot regard the purchase of one share a [*bona fide*] purchase when four are sold simultaneously, that I cannot consider a [*bona fide*] taking-up of one share [any transaction which entails that] ten shares be delivered simultane-ously? . . .

The eighth trick [of the syndicate of the bears] is the following: if it is of im-portance to spread a piece of news which has been invented by the speculators them-selves, they have a letter written and [arrange to have] the letter dropped as if by chance at the right spot. The finder believes himself to possess a treasure, whereas he has really received a letter of Uriah which will lead him into ruin. On his own initiative, he makes known the contents of the letter to his coterie and points out the reasons which will move the syndicate to sell when it receives news of this kind. And if a storm breaks out on the Exchange that very day, the news seems thus to be confirmed, the suspicion ratified, and the apprehensions explained. . . .

Ninthly, the syndicate encourages a friend whose judgment is esteemed, whose connections are respected, and who has never dealt in shares, to sell one or two lots of stock while the risk of loss is borne by the group. The notion [lying behind this manoeuvre] is the belief that anything new attracts attention, and that therefore the decision of this person [to sell stocks] will produce astonishment and will have im-portant consequences. . . .

The tenth trick [of the syndicate] is to whisper into the ear of an intimate friend

---

[38] The above rendering follows the Spanish original. However, the German translator believes that de la Vega made here a double mistake: he should have written "money" instead of "shares" in the first sentence, and he should have seen that the reference to put and call operations intro-duces an unnecessary, somewhat irrelevant idea.

but loud enough to be heard by those who lie in wait for it) that he should sell if ᴋe wants to make money. . . . "The stones speak," says the prophet, and "the walls ᴋave ears," says the proverb; and our conspirators know this truth to be verified by ᴋxperience. If their secret spreads, their advice [seems to have met] with approval, ᴋnd [when] it becomes obvious that they sell blocks of stock, the walls and the ᴋtones do [appear] to talk; people seek the secret reasons of the [whispered] asserᴋions; one is grateful for the hint; and, as cheating a close friend is thought imposᴋble, the manoeuvre meets with success, the fish take the bait, the net becomes filled, ᴋhe victory is celebrated, and the intention of the ring is very advantageously achieved. 304

Eleventhly, the Contremine [i.e., the syndicate] carries out the following trick in ᴋrder to reach its aim: they are not content to wound their enemies with their ᴋongue, which Jeremiah compares to an arrow, and to fight them with their teeth . . . ᴋnd with arguments. In order to insinuate that their own concern is founded on grave ᴋonsiderations and does not refer exclusively to the situation of the Company, the ᴋears sell government obligations. Thus the bulls are to be made to believe that ᴋiscord is dominating the state and that there is a reason to be alarmed about and ᴋo pay attention to a possible outbreak of war. . . . This recourse to selling long ᴋnd short-term state obligations may seem to be of but small importance for the ᴋusiness [in stocks], but whoever thinks so is in error. . . . Our speculators [i.e., ᴋhe bulls] are paralyzed in their stock dealings, and are bled by their engagements ᴋto protect the market] in state bonds, [all because of a trumped-up allegation of a] ᴋituation perilous to the country, dangers threatening the Company, and a breakᴋown of the share market. 305

Finally, the ring practices a twelfth manoeuvre. In order to be well-informed ᴋbout the tendency of the market, even the bears [before launching their big operaᴋion] begin with purchases and take all items [offered]. If the shares rise in price, ᴋhey pocket the quick profit; if the prices fall, however, they sell at a loss, content ᴋo have ascertained the weakening tendency. Moreover, the interest which the timid ᴋublic takes in their proceedings is already useful to them, since the public thinks ᴋhat conditions must be serious when the speculators sell at a loss. This is one of the ᴋost powerful available stratagems for influencing the wavering elements. If [the ᴋmid souls] see the bears buy, they do not know whether the latter buy in order ᴋo sell later (which in the Exchange language means to "look for powder"), or ᴋhether they buy because they have changed their opinion or given up their position ᴋnd therefore really want to buy. If the Contremine decides upon this dissimulation, ᴋhey offer for the stocks more than the price of the day (what we call "inflating" the ᴋrice). They influence the price in this way in order to sell [short] at the higher ᴋgure and thus to gain in the end. God with one breath breathed life into Adam, ᴋhereas the bears take the life of many people by inflating the price [of the ᴋhares]. . . .

Merchant: Do the poor bulls have no means [of defense] against these manoeuvres?

Shareholder: They certainly have. There is protection against the most daring ᴋttacks, and even the greatest slyness finds its master. Inasmuch, however, as the ᴋeans employed in the pursuit of either of these objectives is the same — really those ᴋlready traced out in the case of the bears — I fear that the two-sided manoeuvres ᴋand in the same position [as that just described, i.e., subject to moral condemnation]. Therefore in order to avoid prolixity and repetition, I shall pass over in silence the measures taken by the bulls; [instead] I shall tell you only of the practices of a few sly brokers, who, were they not unscrupulous, would find themselves applauded.[39]

A broker, for example, receives an order to sell 20 shares; if a broker for the bulls receives the order, he begins to perspire from fear and to rage with fury, for, if he sells first the shares bought on his own account, he fears that it will become known and that he will be accused [of sharp practice]. If he keeps his own shares and carries out the sale as ordered, he fears a slump in consequence of the sales so that he could dispose of his own shares only at a great loss. Finally he decides to be honest . . . and from mere fear [of discovery] tries to give up his own interests in order to be able to serve better the order entrusted to him. [But] people scent this [kind of] dissimulation; the Contremine is again encouraged; a shouting begins, "There are pirates near the coast"; another shouts, "Such and such a person must have taken a purgative. He sells as much as he can for secret clients"; a third says, "He is troubled with diarrhoea"; another jests, "He lays eggs"; and all unanimously declare, "He is poisoning the Exchange." These are the expressions which our speculators use in such incidents and which are customary on these occasions. All this does not impress the taciturn broker, for, as he carries out his order to the best of his ability, he will [merely] consider it annoying that the order became known before its execution. But this is a pain which does not go very deeply. As it does not pierce his heart, he feels like a benefactor who causes no losses. . . .

315   The broker in question was doing business on his own account because he expected a rich profit. If [in such a situation] he gets an order, the carrying-out of which binds him in a direction contrary to his own transactions, his heart trembles, his appearance changes, his language becomes heated, his throat goes tight, the voice becomes frightened, the breath stops, and unless he is . . . skillful in escaping from danger . . . , he perishes wretchedly and dies as a fool. . . . In order to avoid this, our broker sells his own shares secretly. He tries to kill the snake around a man's neck without hurting the man; he seeks to avoid the damage [to his own interests] without acting harmfully as far as the specific order is concerned. It would be better to avoid these troubles and to save the pressures on one's heart [by trading only for clients]. What use is it to him to earn something (provided he earns anything at all) if, with the forfeiture of his reputation, he loses his brokerage business and, with the loss of the latter, he is deprived of his fortune? . . .

317   It is even more noteworthy if an unselfish broker endeavors to carry out a large order wisely and cleverly. For, if he tries to buy . . . , all his efforts are directed toward acquiring some shares quickly with the hope that by fortunate bargaining he may secure the rest afterwards [at a reasonable price]. In order to conceal his intentions, he sometimes offers a batch [of shares], and sometimes he asks for offers. If shares are then thrust at him, his purpose has met with success. If one tries to take shares from him, he has [in effect] already bought [the lot that he was charged to buy]; and, without affecting the price [on the Exchange] he obtains double the brokerage fee.[40] He thrusts his sword about with most admirable agility

[39] In this section, de la Vega has reference to the so-called "free" brokers, who participate in the speculation on their own accounts.

[40] Presumably the broker is allowed to charge his principal for the spurious offer to sell, withdrawn at the instance of the principal, as well as for the purchase order that was really executed.

and gives such a pleasing performance that one regrets that he is not always successful. . . .

Ingenuity and audacity [on the part of the broker] are able [at times] to achieve success even if the circumstances of the Exchange are unfavorable, a success which becomes thus all the more admirable.

Again, if a broker, who on his own account is already speculating for a decline, receives an order for a sale, well, there is nothing which equals the joyful mood of such a broker.

Our speculators frequent certain places which are called *coffy-huysen* or coffee-houses because a certain beverage is served there called *coffy* by the Dutch and *Caffé* by the Levantines. The well-heated rooms offer in winter a comfortable place to stay, and there is no lack of manifold entertainment. You will find books and board games, and you will meet there with visitors with whom you can discuss affairs. One person takes chocolate, the others coffee, milk, and tea; and nearly everybody smokes while conversing. None of this occasions very great expense; and while one learns the news, he negotiates and closes transactions.   321

When a bull enters such a coffee-house during the Exchange hours, he is asked the price of the shares by the people present. He adds one to two per cent to the price of the day and he produces a notebook in which he pretends to put down orders. The desire to buy shares increases; and this enhances also the apprehension that there may be a further rise (for on this point we are all alike: when the prices rise, we think that they fly up high and, when they have risen high, that they will run away from us). Therefore, purchase orders are given to the cunning broker.   322 But, in order slyly to reach his own objectives, he replies that he has so many other orders that he cannot be at anyone else's disposal. The naive questioner believes in the sincerity of the statement; his desire to buy becomes even more ardent; and he gives an unrestricted order to another broker. As soon as this becomes known to the sly [first] fellow, the latter hurries to the Exchange and offers the shares at more than the day's price. The other broker, previously uninterested, buys at the higher price because he believes there to be new reasons making for the change in the price and enhancing the desire for investment. At times the increase in the price is maintained, deception has been crowned with success, and what seemed originally as madness comes to have the appearance of cleverness. . . .

One of the neatest tricks which take place in these circles is for some of the   323 bulls to pose as bears. This is done for two reasons. First, because the opponents [the real bears] imagine that, if they [are able to] buy a share from among those held back and concealed, the other party [that of the bulls] has changed its ideas and, instead of building silver bridges for them, seek to drag them down. . . . Now the bulls change the price so that they [the bears] are forced to pay dearly for the shares which they have sold short [in their attempt to subdue the bulls]. Thus the bulls reach their aim, and thus they defeat their malevolent enemies through presence, and thus by cautious manoeuvres they deceive these opponents who are trying to deceive them.

Secondly, these speculators resort to such a trick in order, in sudden conjunctures, to sell without producing a panic. As it is taken for granted that these [particular] speculators undoubtedly belong to the Contremine, the bulls rally around furiously in order to buy the shares offered by the first group, on the assumption that they have to stand by their opinions and have to make sacrifices for them.

One man [a broker] tries to find out what is happening in an assemblage on the Exchange. Therefore he puts his head through the arms of the persons forming the group (quite unmindful of the unpleasant smells of perspiration), and learns that eight [588] is offered for the shares without anybody agreeing to that price. The broker then turns away, and joins the group from the other side, pretending to have heard nothing, and to have a purchase order without restriction as to price. He begins to bid eight and a half; his followers screw up courage and offer nine; and finally this brings success, causing exultation and winning applause. If an electric eel is placed among dead fish, the latter make movements again when pushed about by its contortions. The bulls [similarly] seem to be dead before they are awakened and revived by this broker through his voice, through his lies, and through his courage. Everything he undertakes is done in an energetic and mercurial fashion, and this lively and vivacious rogue can even effect a resurrection of the dead. When at the sight of the wolf the cattle become silent, and the frog takes on a pale color the moment it is looked at, how wonderful it is that even the bears become silent and grow pale on such an occasion? . . .

There are three [commonly used] formulas by which a purchase or sale of shares can be initiated. [A seller states], "I give them to you at this price"; or he says, "I give them at that price" without further explanation. Or you say, "I give them at this price to everybody who wants to have them." [In addition, there are formulas not commonly employed because they are so dangerous.] Whoever says [merely], "I give them," has no escape from delivering at any price on demand; and if this person, later regretting his bargain, is not liberated from his obligation out of friendship, there is nothing left for him to do except to pray, complain, and suffer. Whoever says, "I give them to anybody who wants them," exposes himself to a great danger, for there are people who count on such a broad offer, as if their daily bread depended on it. Since the status, the insignificant capital, the low reputation, and the limited trustworthiness of such people are well known, they do not dare attempt to carry on any considerable business. But if they hear of such a generous offer as that made by our braggart, they rapidly disconcert him by shouting, "They are mine!" Thus he is punished for his [excess of] confidence, and he lives to repent his rashness.

He who says merely, "I give," does so with an equivocal aim. . . . For his wish is not to sell but to cause the prices to move. If there is someone who expressed a desire to buy, [the dealer's] prompt answer is, "I give, but not to you," and, as he cannot be obligated to anything else because — strictly speaking — he had said only, "I give," he is always fighting with a two-edged sword and a double-barrelled pistol.

I am not surprised that there are brokers who (if their names are well enough known) countersign their contracts, "N.N. by order." They are tempted to act like this by an eagerness to deal on their own accounts, and they choose this kind of countersignature to suggest that the business is done only on "order" of a customer. Thus they understand how to cloak their avarice and to screen their foolishness.

325

I am more surprised that already for a long time some enterprising brokers have run [two establishments], one for true brokerage and another for Exchange transactions on their own accounts. At the delivery of the stocks they have designated themselves as principals, and promoted the idea that a change in the name meant an actual change. A man with his wife tried to pay in a public house for only one person by reference to the words of God that man and wife were of one flesh. But when the landlord realized that they utilized sophistry to his detriment, he made efforts to repay them in their own coin and demanded that the two should pay for eleven, for, if two were one, then the number one put twice side by side is eleven. It seems that the strategem of the artful brokers is in conformity with the shrewdness of the landlord, for each of them tries to imagine that he can occupy five places, playing at the same time the role of broker, merchant, contractor, lawyer, and judge. . . .

333

It is with reason, however, that [any] faction of the Exchange is in dismay when the most influential and most respected of their brokers, under whose protection they have been standing, leave them. Such a broker serves (we can assume) the most select, wealthiest, and most enterprising people of the Exchange. The bulls are his customers; and the pursuit of his principals' best interests is ever the object of his even-handed zeal. One day an ingenious bear recognizes that the price of stocks is beginning to waver. In order to stimulate a more rapid fall of the price, he gives an [honest] broker an order to sell ten shares without revealing the name of his principal. The broker carries out the order honestly, cleverly, and discreetly because all he wants is to earn the brokerage fee, although he is obviously causing damage to his friends [the bulls]. His followers are amazed, and he is asked whether he is selling for patrons. They ask him whether he has any recent news. He gives no answer. They want to know whether he has to sell many shares. He is silent. Therefore his former followers, (furious about his change of heart and his treason), in order to cause him trouble and to prevent him from arranging a profitable sale, cause the prices to rise, accusing him of ingratitude in leaving their advantage out of consideration. When the truth is revealed which had been ingeniously concealed, the bear who gave the order has already attained his objective, he has sown disharmony, has caused the prices to change, and can boast of his complete success. . . .

Numerous [brokers] are inexhaustible in inventing [involved manoeuvres], but for just this reason do not achieve their purposes. The bulls spread a thousand rumors about the stocks, of which one would be enough to force up the prices. A thousand stratagems of the Contremine are launched in an effort to cause ill-temper on the exchange. If by chance, however, some of the fabrications come to be confirmed, the real situation may turn out to be of less consequence [than one might anticipate]. If it becomes known, for instance, that a situation is not as favorable as one feared, the prices rise in spite of a deterioration of the situation. On the other hand, a decline [of values may] set in when a propitious event falls short of expectations.

When a cunning broker [interested in a price rise] has to buy two thousand pounds [worth of shares], he first buys but one thousand pounds [worth] in order to convey the impression that he will take [stocks worth] at least twenty [thousand] pounds. As soon as he sees that another [broker] buys too, whether to follow his example or to flatter him, he approaches the latter and talks to him in a hushed voice expressing anguish (but audibly enough to be heard by those who make efforts to catch his remarks). He implores the other for Heaven's sake not to ruin him and not to influence the prices, for he has still to take care of a tremendous volume, and if there were a disturbance the transaction would be a failure, and a loss inevitable. Now the Exchange takes as a serious endeavor what is only a ruse. Immediately everyone begins to buy in order to secure the profit which, according to the [presumed] tendency, is to be expected. Though the success of this trick is not wholly certain, it is often worth trying. The evil spirit gave the advice to Eve to eat from the Forbidden Tree that she might become immortal. If this had been possible, the evil spirit would not have given his advice, for he gave advice only for his own advantage. It is just the same with the actions of the evil spirits on our

338   Exchange. If, however, they try — as described above — to persuade their friends not to buy shares in order to buy them themselves and if, in asking the friends not to influence the prices, they [act in a manner] themselves that alters prices, such an artifice possesses something almost divine. . . .

When a generous broker wants to favor a relative, he [may have to] approach him a hundred times before he is able [actually] to give the necessary information without being overheard by those who lie in wait for [such presumably choice] data. From fear of this contingency . . . , abbreviated words are used, and from this expediency misunderstandings ensue, because often the opposite of what was

339   intended is understood. One day I asked a gentleman who was busily engaged on his own affairs what in his opinion was likely to happen. He answered excitedly, "Ven." [41] I thought he called me; I followed him, and saw that he bought many shares at a public house without telling me anything else. So I assumed that "Ven" meant that I should follow him, and the purchases signified that I should also buy. Highly satisfied with the suggestions, I hurried to the Exchange, and bought there a small batch of shares, when I suddenly noticed that my adviser sold eight shares in one lot. Offended [at this apparent perfidy], I complained that he had invited me to join his operation and that he had deceived me in a very offensive manner. But he assured me (actually confirming this assertion by further sales) that he had used the shares acquired secretly merely to shake the position of his enemies. He said that he had also advised me sufficiently that I should sell by telling me repeatedly, "Ven," and that he could not have uttered it more distinctly lest someone should have heard it. . . .

342   Despicable meanness is the appropriate characterization of the practice of [a few]
343   brokers who (concealing their real intentions under the appearance of complaisance) act in the following manner even though they are thought dishonorable for doing so, namely, they advise an intimate friend to sell, despite the fact that they have a purchase order. Even worse, they cause the sale of shares which they themselves through somebody else have pressed on the person concerned, as if it were not very easy to deceive an unsuspecting person. . . .

353   *Merchant*: We ask you to reward our attention only by telling us the reason of

---

[41] *Ven* is a conspicuous element in the Spanish words *venir* and *vender*, meaning "come" and "sell."

he [recent] unheard-of collapse in the price of the shares, which spelled such a deplorable crash in so short a time.

Shareholder: Yes, I shall do so with great pleasure. That you may listen more calmly I will mention that the price has risen again to 465 from the 365 to which the shares had fallen, and is holding at this level. But be aware of the many traps which the evil spirit has laid in the path of the bulls. . . . In the book of Job, the evil spirit says to God that he has roamed over the earth. I believe that before our misfortune [this same evil spirit] visited the sea and the land, since unfavorable news arrived from both hither and yon and constituted the starting point of the fatal events. On land there was peace and calm everywhere; on the Exchange, a goodly supply of money and abundant credit were available; there were splendid prospects for exports; a vigorous spirit of enterprise [manifested itself]; brilliant military forces under famous leaders were [protecting the country]; there was favorable news, incomparable knowledge of business, a swelling population, a strong fleet, advantageous alliances. Therefore not the slightest concern, not the least apprehension reigned, not the smallest cloud, not the most fleeting shadow was to be seen.

354

By sea a letter arrived from the governor of the Cape of Good Hope (which was delivered by French ships). The letter contained the news that in India things were going on as everyone would wish and that the ships from India had arrived [at the Cape] with the richest of cargoes. These fortunate circumstances were explained partly by the opening of the Chinese market and partly by the discovery of new mines. At any rate, everyone anticipated good harvests and a favorable economic situation. In wide circles a miracle was expected, so great as to surprise everybody.

Only one circumstance ran counter to these promising prospects. This was the news that one of the most heavily laden ships had returned from the Cape to Batavia because she had not been able to continue her voyage by reason of a dangerous list. But even this annoyance was lightly regarded since it was assumed that this ship would sail with the *Naa Schepen*, that is, two or three smaller ships departing from Batavia some months after the first which generally brought cargoes to the value of four tons [of gold] as well as the books, accounts, and balance sheets of the East Indian administration for the use of the directors [in the Netherlands]. A few days before the arrival of the first squadron, [a different but] apparently quite reliable report was spread that this squadron had run aground on a sandbank but was out of danger; and further that the ship that had turned back had actually sailed in the convoy of the fleet. Such news, agreeable to the bulls and important as far as dividends were concerned, aroused the spirit of Ahab and Satan [on the Exchange]. Everybody who did not join in the jubilation was regarded as a fool, and everyone who sold shares was looked at as a tenacious and deadly enemy of his own interests, each sale being called foolishness, madness, and a crime.

The ships arrived safely in the harbor, and the directors read part of the incoming letters. When it was rumored that the freight (of the goods purchased [in India] called *Inkoop*) amounted to the value of only 34 tons [of gold] compared with 50 tons last year, the mood changed and optimism ceased. But the blow could not have been so severe if the Contremine had not speculated on a rise too. Baffled by the magnificent prospects, they had not dared to wage a battle. Had the Contremine sold [short] a goodly number of shares, it would have had sufficient advantage, when prices fell 20 per cent in the first movement, [to have bought stock to cover its commitments], and would have pocketed the profit. The collapse of prices [in the whole crash] would not have been so violent. But, as some people wanted to sell in order not to lose still more [than they already stood to lose], others to avoid any loss at all, others again in order still to gain something, the selling became general, and dejection supervened everywhere. Those who were compelled to take delivery [of shares contracted for earlier], sold again in order to be able to cover their obligations. He who was in the possession of hypothecated shares sold them because their value had sunk under the amount of the sum borrowed [to carry them]. He who had bought sold lest he should lose even more, and sold still more in order to make up for the [earlier] loss. The few sellers who had already sold short [purposefully] caused a further fall of the prices, encouraged by the prospect of a profit and seeking to exploit their luck. In the end people went begging with the shares [as it were], as if one asked alms of the [prospective] purchaser. Such a panic, such an inexplicable shock was produced that the whole world seemed to crumble, the earth to be submerged, and the heavens to fall.

The general atmosphere began to improve when the contents of a second series of Company letters were made known. It appeared that by the sale of the 34 tons [of this year's import] just as much could be gained [because of the higher prices] as from the 50 tons of the year before. So the bears crowded together and, in order not to let the bulls take breath, spread the rumor that a war would break out. [They said that] they knew of so many secret preparatory measures that no doubt could be entertained. Then the taxes would increase like an avalanche, the burdens would grow immeasurably, the whole of Europe would be set ablaze, and misery, terror, and ruin would be found everywhere. Even those were alarmed who already had a notion of the scheme projected by the Contremine. [Consequently], the bears were able exclusively to control the market prices. To such an extent were they the masters of the situation that they refrained from selling shares against cash, merely to avoid a suspension of payments, wishing to have a few solvent people left. Thus the stock exchange came into the sad plight that I have just described; and even a few persons who were regarded as quite substantial sought the shelter provided for over-extended purchasers of options [they appealed to the decree of Frederick Henry]. Here the wise saying is confirmed that like Saul you often seek David in his bed and find only a statue. On the Exchange, too, one found stones instead of men, and its strongest supporters collapsed like thin sticks.

In the ducaton speculation the damage was still more disturbing. (Speculation [in these imaginary units] was declared by court decisions to be a game or a bet and thus the transactions in them were denied the character of true business.) Therefore it was not even necessary to appeal to Frederick Henry's decree in order to refuse payment.

When, in this pocket-picking, each 500 pounds [worth of stock, equal to 3,000 gulden] was diminished 300 gulden and afterwards 500 gulden, the speculator behaved in quite variant ways. A few men of honor paid everything, and others at least a part, as far as their fortunes went. But there were also persons who, under the influence of the sudden suspension of business (of which no one spoke any more), paid nothing, but they demanded nothing either. One group of brokers lid not pay because of complete insolvency; again others had to refuse payments as their business connections became weak and their resources did not suffice. There were even people who boasted of their suspension of payments and who possessed the objectionable brazenness to say that they made money out of dirt in order to cheat their creditors. If these men had been polite instead of impudent, they would have said at least that man is made of dust, and, as they could do nothing else for the satisfaction of their creditors, they gave what they were themselves, namely, dust, and thus would offer their bodies instead of other sacrifices. . . .

[As things turned out], the importations [of the East India Company] yielded an exceedingly fine result. But here . . . the light was hidden as in a jug [as was true of Gideon's army]. Only the quantities imported, but not their values, were known. The bold speculators (as I told you) did not see the splendor of the transactions but only the *cover* which hid the latter. After the examination of the latest business letters [from India], it turned out that the sale of the cargoes was to yield excellent revenues. The vessel broke, and the light became visible, but at the same moment the bears sounded the trumpet, and shouted that war would be declared.

What a terrible cruelty it was that these destroyers of the Exchange made pass for an accomplished fact not only what was going to happen, but even things that could only *possibly* occur! The bears foresaw that [under certain circumstances] the United Provinces would wage war, and this presumption was a sufficient basis for them to proclaim the outbreak of the war. Yet I am not surprised at [their forecast], but at the fact that, in the mere possibility of the war, they saw the outbreak already certain. . . .

This, my friends, is all that I have to say about the [late] misfortunes on the stock exchange, although my presentation gives only a pale picture of the events. . . .

Everyone was involved in the speculation. When it began, the Exchange presented a rosy picture; when it ended, a sad one. . . . The watchword *Audaces fortuna juvat* . . . has no validity relative to the [East India] Company for we see that from trading in its shares the audacious did not win but were prostrated.

In spite of these difficulties, [however] I advise you to speculate for a rise and not for a fall. The sincerity of my words is confirmed by the circumstance that I recommend something that has caused me losses, and that I think good something that has ruined me. I advise you well just because of my misfortune. . . . And, that you may see that a revival of the stock exchange has already been brought about, I draw your attention to the fact that the shares which had gone down by 180 per cent because of the apprehension of an outbreak of the war have risen again by 100 per cent [of the face value] since its declaration. . . .

What makes me especially sad is the sudden end of the ducaton speculation, on which so many decent people and so many men with small means subsisted. For this tree had sunk so many roots that nobody thought the trunk likely to fall in the first storm, and the high prices suddenly to decline. . . . Sad indeed is a catastrophe that annihilates at one stroke names, dreams, persons, fortunes, and reputations.

Julius Caesar made use of aid from the mathematician Sosigenes to alter the inconstant lunar year into the constant astronomical year of 365 days 6 hours, and to fix the equinox on always the same day. As it was necessary to alter the dates

377

of all festive days . . . and to put in two intercalary months, the year of transition was ordinarily called the *Year of Confusion*. The ducaton speculators realized that on the first of September the liquidation of their transactions had to be completed. They, too, desired an astronomer to change the seasons and wished that the September [settlement] be prolonged until November in order to see whether a recovery of prices would occur and whether their anxiety could be ended. But though they did not secure that aim, the same effect was reached as with the alteration of the calendar. This year too was a *year of confusion* for many unlucky speculators declared in one voice that the present crisis was the labyrinth of labyrinths, the terror of terrors, the *confusion of confusions*. . . .

I suspend this discourse because agonies disturb my spirit. I request you to accept, as an indication of my friendship, the affection with which I have described to you the progress of this famous Company which, after certain ships had initiated voyages in 1594, was founded in 1602 (as I pointed out to you) by order of the States General, and which, despite the extensive oppositions of the Portuguese and the Spaniards, could enjoy (such as it does enjoy) the conquest of so many kingdoms and the tribute of so many kings. . . .

On geographical maps fine dotted lines are drawn around undiscovered regions which are named *Terra incognita*. On the Exchange, too, there are many secret operations which I have not been able to discover, but I make use of the trick of the geographers; until new investigations shall grant you knowledge, I have pointed out the objects to you by means of thin lines. I hope that as friends you will excuse the shortcomings of the presentation and as educated men compensate for my errors.

Merchant: I on my part thank you for the instruction. I esteem business but hate gambling. I have a notion that my faculties do not suffice for such complicated transactions. If I nearly lost my sense when I wanted to learn about the speculations, you may conclude of what importance to me is the conduct of Exchange transactions. It is possible that I shall become a holder of shares and shall deal [in shares] in an honest way, but I am very sure that I shall never become a speculator. . . .

Philosopher: I will take the same course because I am too old to defy dangers and to endure storms. I shall keep my shares until it shall please God that [after the recent downfall of the prices] I can get out of them in peace, for I will only save myself and not gather wealth. . . . All schools of philosophy teach that the soul is nobler than the body, life nobler than death, and the existent nobler than the nonexistent. But, as for the stock exchange, I approve the paradoxical opinion of the Platonic musician that the non-existent is better than the existent. I think it much better not to be a speculator, [and in making that statement] I have in mind real speculation, not the honest business in shares, for what is fair in the latter is dubious in the former. . . .

CPSIA information can be obtained at www.ICGtesting.com
Printed in the USA
BVOW07s0820270415

397207BV00013B/144/P